OF NEW ENGLAND

OF NEW ENGLAND

HANS HOLZER

YANKEE BOOKS

CAMDEN • MAINE

Stories published in other publications:

"Haunted Is the Trailer," *Psychic Investigator,* New York: Hawthorne Books, 1968.

"Ghosts around Boston," *The Ghost Hunter's Strangest Cases,* New York: Ace, 1975.

"The Possession of Mrs. F." and "The Strange Case of the Late but Lively Husband," *Possessed,* New York: Fawcett, 1973.

"A New Hampshire Artist and Her Ghost," *The Lively Ghosts of Ireland,* New York: Bobbs-Merrill, 1967.

"The Ghosts of Stamford Hill" and "The Ghosts at Morris-Jumel Mansion," *Ghosts I've Met,* New York: Bobbs-Merrill, 1966.

"The Haunted Organ at Yale," *Where the Ghosts Are,* New York: Parker, 1984.

"The Terror on the Farm" and "The Old Merchant's House," *Gothic Ghosts,* New York: Bobbs-Merrill, 1966.

Designed by Margo Letourneau

First Edition

Copyright 1989 by Hans Holzer

Holzer, Hans, 1920-

    Ghosts of New England.

    1. Ghosts — New England.   2. Ghosts — New York (State)

  I. Title.

BF1472.U6H6374   1988   133.1'0974   88-27777

ISBN 0-89909-151-2

ISBN 0-89909-222-5

Third Printing

Contents

Preface

In this collection culled from my best and most exciting cases of true ghost stories and hauntings in the New England and New York states, I am once again demonstrating that ghosts know neither time nor place when it comes to reliving their own personal and often painfully emotional traumas.

To people caught between two states of being, which is what ghosts are, the events of their last moments in the physical world have never ceased and the solution continues to escape them.

The people who report these experiences are neither fanciful nor demented but ordinary citizens of a very real world. But so are the ghosts they report: it is just that the two dimensions differ though they coexist.

In this age where so-called Channeling — the alleged ability to speak with the personality of a long-gone master — has become popular, without so much as the need for evidence that these entities ever existed in the real world, it is comforting to know that the spectral communicators of *Ghosts of New England* were all real people with lives in this world when they were still in their physical bodies. Anything less than that kind of reasonable evidence invites uncritical belief in something that cannot really be proven.

If there seem to be, at times, inconsistencies or discrepancies in the transcript of what a medium will say clairvoyantly or in trance, bear in mind that this is a less than perfect means of communication between two very different worlds. In parapsychology we record what is being said *faithfully,* not what reads nicely in a book. We do not editorialize but report what comes through. This is as it should be, if we are to present an accurate picture, not of what the story or case ultimately may be but what our method of research consists of.

We try to verify as many facts, names, and statements made by sensitives as possible; we never succeed in getting them all verified simply because the nature of the transmission is at best, imperfect, and also because the records and documents available to me as a trained professional historian and researcher are far from complete. Just because a statement cannot be verified in a printed source, or a letter, or some other document in the files of a library or other learned institution, does not mean the statement is false; it merely means we have not been able to find that particular verification.

The ghostly encounters I have presented here are all cases I have personally looked into and investigated. I am satisfied that they are true cases of life beyond physical death.

Prof. Hans Holzer, Ph. D.
New York, New York
January 1988

The Ghost Who Would Not Leave

Hardly had I finished investigating the rather colorful haunting in the New York State home of *Newsday* columnist Jack Altschul, which resulted in my name appearing in his column as a man who goes around chasing ghosts, than I heard from a gentleman, now deceased, who was the public relations director of the Sperry Company and a man not ordinarily connected with specters.

Ken Brigham wanted me to know that he had a resident ghost at his summer home in Maine, and what was I to do about it. He assured me that while the lady ghost he was reporting was not at all frightening to him and his family, he would, nevertheless, prefer she went elsewhere. This is a sentiment I have found pervasive with most owners of haunted property, and while it shows a certain lack of sentimentality, it is a sound point of view even from the ghost's perspective because being an earthbound spirit really has no future, so to speak.

All this happened in January of 1967. I was keenly interested. At the time, I was working closely with the late Ethel Johnson

Meyers, one of the finest trance mediums ever, and it occurred to me immediately that, if the case warranted it, I would get her involved in it.

I asked Mr. Brigham, as is my custom, to put his report in writing, so I could get a better idea as to the nature of the haunting. He did this with the precision expected from a public relations man representing a major instrument manufacturer. Here then is his initial report:

> As a member of the public relation/advertising profession, I've always been considered a cynical, phlegmatic individual and so considered myself. I'm not superstitious, walk under ladders, have never thought about the "spirit world," am not a deeply religious person, etc., but . . .
>
> Eight years ago, my wife and I purchased, for a summer home, a nonworking farm in South Waterford, Maine. The ten-room farmhouse had been unoccupied for two years prior to our acquisition. Its former owners were an elderly couple who left no direct heirs and who had been virtually recluses in their latter years. The house apparently was built in two stages; the front part about 1840, and the ell sometime around 1800. The ell contains the original kitchen and family bedroom; a loft overhead was used during the nineteenth century for farm help and children. The former owners for many years occupied only a sitting room, the kitchen, and a dining room; all other rooms being closed and shuttered. The so-called sitting room was the daily and nightly abode. We never met the Bells, both of whom died of old age in nursing homes in the area, several years before we purchased the farm. They left it to relatives; all the furniture was auctioned off.
>
> The first summer my wife and I set about restoring the

farmhouse. The old kitchen became our livingroom; the Bell's sitting room became another bedroom; the old dining room, our kitchen. One bright noontime, I was painting in the new livingroom. All the doors were open in the house. Aware that someone was looking at me, I turned toward the bedroom door and there, standing in bright sunlight, was an elderly woman; she was staring at me. Dressed in a matronly housedress, her arms were folded in the stance common to many housewives. I was startled, thinking she must have entered the house via the open front door and had walked through the front sitting room to the now-bedroom. Behind her eyeglasses, she maintained a passive, inquisitive expression. For a moment or two, we stared at each other. I thought, What do you say to a native who has walked through your house, without sounding unneighborly? and was about to say something like What can I do for you? when she disappeared. She was there and then she wasn't. I hurried through the bedrooms and, of course, there was no one.

Once or twice that summer I was awakened by a sudden, chill draft passing through the second-floor room we used as a master bedroom. One early evening, while I was taking a shower, my wife called me from the livingroom with near-panic in her voice. I hurried downstairs as quickly as possible only to have her ask if I intended to remain downstairs.

Before closing the house up for the winter, I casually described the apparition to local friends without disclosing my reasons, excusing the inquiry from a standpoint I was interested in the previous owners. Apparently my description was accurate, for our friends wanted to know where I'd seen Mrs. Bell; I had difficulty passing it off.

My wife wasn't put off, however, and later that evening we compared notes for the first time. The night she called me, she explained, she had felt a cold draft pass behind her and had looked up toward the door of the former sitting room (which was well lighted). There, in the door, was the clear and full shadow of a small woman. My wife then cried out to me. The chill breeze went through the room and the shadow disappeared. My wife reported, however, that surprisingly enough she felt a sense of calm. No feeling of vindictiveness.

Over the years, we've both awakened spontaneously to the chill draft and on more than one occasion have watched a pinpoint light dance across the room. The house is isolated and on a private road, discounting any possible headlights, etc. After a moment or so, the chill vanishes.

A couple of times, guests have queried us on hearing the house creak or on hearing footsteps, but we pass these off.

The summer before last, however, our guests' reaction was different.

A couple with two small children stayed with us. The couple occupied the former sitting room, which now is furnished as a Victorian-style bedroom with a tremendous brass bed. Their daughter occupied another first-floor bedroom, and their son shared our son's bedroom on the second floor. A night light was left on in the latter bedroom and in the bathroom, thereby illuminating the upper hallway, and, dimly, the lower hallway. My wife and I occupied another bedroom on the second floor that is our custom.

During the early hours of the morning, we were awakened by footsteps coming down the upper hallway.

They passed our door, went into the master bedroom, paused, continued into our room and after a few minutes, passed on and down the staircase. My wife called out, thinking it was one of the boys, possibly ill. No answer. The chill breeze was present, and my wife again saw the woman's shadow against the bedroom wall. The children were sound asleep.

In the morning, our adult guests were quiet during breakfast, and it wasn't until later that the woman asked if we'd been up during the night and had come downstairs. She'd been awakened by the footsteps and by someone touching her arm and her hair. Thinking it was her husband, she found him soundly sleeping. In the moonlight, she glanced toward a rocking chair in the bedroom and said she was certain someone had moved it and the clothes left on it. She tried to return to sleep, but again was awakened, certain someone was in the room, and felt someone move the blanket and touch her arm.

My wife and I finally acknowledged our "ghost," but our woman guest assured us that she felt no fright, to her own surprise, and ordinarily wouldn't have believed such "nonsense," except that I, her host, was too "worldly" to be a spiritualist.

At least one other guest volunteered a similar experience.

Finally I admitted my story to our local friends, asking them not to divulge the story in case people thought we were "kooks." But I asked them if they would locate a photograph of the Bell family. Needless to say, the photograph they located was identical with my apparition. An enlargement now is given a prominent place in our livingroom.

Although this experience hasn't frightened us with the

house, it has left us puzzled. My wife and I both share the feeling that "whatever [it is] is more curious than unpleasant; more interested than destructive.

I was impressed and replied we would indeed venture Down East. It so happened that Catherine, whom I was married to at the time, and I were doing some traveling in upper New Hampshire that August, and Ethel Johnson Meyers was vacationing at Lake Sebago. All that needed to be done was coordinate our travel plans and set the date.

Mr. Brigham, who then lived in Great Neck, New York, was delighted and gave us explicit instructions on how to traverse New Hampshire from Pike, New Hampshire, where I was lecturing at the Lake Tarleton Club, to our intended rendezvous with Ethel in Bridgton, Maine, at the Cumberland Hotel. The date we picked was August 14, 1967. Ken and Doris Brigham then suggested we could stay over at the haunted house, if necessary, and I assured them that I doubted the need for it, being a bit cocksure of getting through to, and rid of, the ghost all in the same day.

* * *

Crossing the almost untouched forests from New Hampshire to Maine on a road called the Kancamagus Highway was quite an experience for us: we rode for a very, very long time without ever seeing a human habitation, or, for that matter, a gas station. But then the Indians whose land this was never worried about such amenities.

Before we left, we had received a brief note from Ken Brigham about the existence of this road cutting through the White Mountains. He also informed me that some of the witnesses to the phenomena at the house would be there for our visit, and I would have a chance to meet them, including Mrs. Mildred Haynes Noyes, a neighbor who was able to identify the ghostly apparition for the Brighams. Most of the phenomena had occurred in the livingroom, downstairs in the house, as well as in the long central hall, and in one upper-story front bedroom as well, Mr. Brigham added.

At the time I had thought of bringing a television documentary crew along to record the investigations, but it never worked out that way, and in the end I did some filming myself and sound recorded the interviews, and, of course, Ethel Meyers's trance.

When we finally arrived at the house in question in Waterford, Maine, Ethel had no idea where she was exactly or why. She never asked questions when I called on her skills. Directly on arrival she began pacing up and down in the grounds adjacent to the house as if to gather up her bearings. She often did that, and I followed her around with my tape recorder like a dog follows its master.

"I see a woman at the window, crying," she suddenly said and pointed to an upstairs window. "She wears a yellow hat and dress. There is a dog with her. Not from this period. Looking out, staring at something."

We then proceeded to enter the house and found ourselves in a very well appointed livingroom downstairs; a fire in the fireplace gave it warmth, even though this was the middle of August. The house and all its furnishings were kept as much as possible in the Federal period style, and one had the feeling of having suddenly stepped back into a living past.

When we entered the adjacent dining room, Ethel pointed at one of the tall windows and informed us that the lady was still standing there.

"Dark brown eyes, high cheekbones, smallish nose, now she has pushed back the bonnet hat, dark reddish-brown hair," Ethel intoned. I kept taking photographs pointing the camera toward the area where Ethel said the ghost was standing. The pictures did not show anything special, but then Ethel was not a photography medium, someone who has that particular phase of mediumship. I asked Ethel to assure the woman we had come in friendship and peace, to help her resolve whatever conflict might still keep her here.

I asked Ethel to try to get the woman's name. Ethel seemed to listen, then said, "I like to call her Isabelle, Isabelle . . . "

"How is she connected to the house?"

"Lived here."

I suggested that Ethel inform the woman we wanted to talk to her. Earnestly, Ethel then addressed the ghost, assuring her of no harm. Instead of being comforted, Ethel reported, the woman just kept on crying.

We asked the ghost to come with us as we continued the tour of the house; we would try and have her communicate through Ethel in trance somewhere in the house where she could be comfortable. Meanwhile Ethel gathered further psychic impressions as we went from room to room.

"Many layers here . . . three layers . . . men fighting and dying here . . . " she said. "Strong Indian influence also . . . then there is a small child here . . . later period . . . the men have guns, bleeding . . . no shoes . . . pretty far back . . . Adam . . . Joseph . . . Balthazar . . . war victims . . . house looks different . . . they're lying around on the floor, in pain . . . some kind of skirmish has gone on here."

I decided to chase the lady ghost again. We returned to the livingroom. Ethel picked a comfortable chair and prepared herself for the trance that would follow.

"I get the names Hattie . . . and Martin . . . not the woman at the window . . . early period . . . connected with the men fighting . . . not in house, outside . . . Golay? Go-something . . . it is their house. They are not disturbed but they give their energy to the other woman. Someone by the name of Luther comes around. Someone is called Marygold . . . Mary . . . someone says, the house is all different."

I decided to stop Ethel recounting what may well have been psychic impressions from the past rather than true ghosts, though

Ghosts of New England

one cannot always be sure of that distinction. But my experience has taught me that the kind of material she had picked up sounded more diffuse, more fractional than an earthbound spirit would be.

"Abraham . . . , " Ethel mumbled and slowly went into deep trance as we watched. The next voice we would hear might be her guide, Albert's, who usually introduces other entities to follow, or it might be a stranger — but it certainly would not be Ethel's.

"It's a man. Abram . . . Ibram . . . , " she said, breathing heavily. I requested her guide Albert's assistance in calming the atmosphere.

Ethel's normally placid face was now totally distorted as if in great pain and her hands were at her throat, indicating some sort of choking sensation; with this came unintelligible sounds of ah's and o's. I continued to try and calm the transition.

I kept asking who the communicator was, but the moaning continued, at the same time the entity now controlling Ethel indicated that the neck or throat had been injured as if by hanging or strangulation. Nevertheless, I kept up my request for identification, as I always do in such cases, using a quiet, gentle vocal approach and reassurances that the pain was of the past and only a memory now.

Finally, the entity said his name was Abraham and that he was in much pain.

"Abraham . . . Eben . . . my tongue!" the entity said, and indeed he sounded as if he could not use his tongue properly. Clearly, his tongue had been cut out, and I kept telling him that he was using the medium's now and therefore should be able to speak clearly. But he continued in a way that all I could make out was "my house."

"Is this your house?"

"Yes . . . why do you want to know . . . who are you?"

"I am a friend come to help you. Is this your house?"

"I live here . . . "

"How old are you?"

No answer.

"What year is this?"

"Seventy-eight . . . going on . . . seventy-nine . . . "

"How old are you?"

"Old man . . . fifty-two . . . "

"Where were you born?"

"Massachusetts . . . Lowell . . . "

"Who was it who hurt you?"

Immediately he became agitated again, and the voice became unintelligible, the symptoms of a cutout tongue returned. Once again, I calmed him down.

"What church did you go to?" I asked, changing the subject.

"Don't go to church much . . .," he replied.

"Where were you baptized?"

"St. Francis . . . Episcopal."

I suggested the entity should rest now, seeing that he was getting agitated again, and I also feared for the medium.

"I want justice . . . justice . . .," he said.

I assured him, in order to calm him down, that those who had done him wrong had been punished. But he would have none of it.

"They fight every night out there . . . "

Again, I began to exorcise him, but he was not quite ready.

"My daughter . . . Lisa . . . Elizabeth . . . "

"How old is she?"

"Thirteen . . . she cries for me, she cries for me, she weeps . . . all the blood . . . they take her, too . . . "

"Where is your wife?"

"She left us in misery. Johanna . . . don't mention her . . . she left us in misery."

"What year was that?"

"This year. NOW . . . "

"Why did she leave you?"

"I don't know."

"Where did she go?"

"I don't know."

And he added, "I will go to find her . . . I never see her . . . "

"What about your father and mother? Are they alive?"

"Oh no . . . "

"When did they die?"

"1776"

The voice showed a definite brogue now.

"Where are they buried?"

"Over the water . . . Atlantic Ocean . . . home . . . "

"Where did your people come from?"

"Wales . . . Greenough . . . "

Further questioning brought out he was a captain in the 5th regiment.

"Did you serve the king or the government of the colonies?" I asked. Proudly the answer came.

"The king."

When I asked him for the name of the commanding officer of the regiment he served in, he became agitated and hissed at me . . . "I am an American citizen . . . I'll have you know!"

"Are you a patriot or a Tory?"

"I will not have you use that word," he replied, meaning he was not a Tory.

I went on to explain that time had passed, but he called me mad; then I suggested I had come as a friend, which elicited a bitter reply.

"What are friends in time of war?"

I explained that the war had long been over.

"The war is not over . . . I am an American . . . don't tempt me again . . . "

Once again I pressed him for the name of his commanding

officer and this time we received a clear reply: Broderick. He was not infantry, but horse. We were finally getting some answers. I then asked him for the names of some of his fellow officers in the 5th regiment.

"All dead . . ., " he intoned, and when I insisted on some names, he added, Anthony . . . Murdoch . . . Surgeon . . . my head hurts!"

"Any officers you can remember?"

"Matthew . . . "

I asked, what battles was he involved in.

"Champlain . . . Saint Lawrence . . . it's bad, it's bad . . . "

He was showing signs of getting agitated again, and time was fleeting.

I decided to release the poor tortured soul, asking him whether he was ready to join his loved ones now. Once again he relived the wars.

"He won't come home again . . . Hatteras . . . fire . . . I'm weary."

I began to exorcise him, suggesting he leave the house where he had suffered so much.

"My house . . . my tongue . . . Indians," he kept repeating.

But finally with the help of Ethel's spirit guide (and first husband) Albert, I was able to help him across. Albert, in his crisp voice, explained that one of the female presences in the house, a daughter of the spirit we had just released, might be able to communicate now. But what I was wondering was whether a disturbed earthbound spirit was in the house also, not necessarily a relative of this man. Albert understood, and withdrew, and after a while, a faint, definitely female voice began to come from the medium's still entranced lips.

"Ella . . . " the voice said, faintly at first.

Then she added that she was very happy and had a baby with

her. The baby's name was Lily. She was Ella, she repeated. When I asked as to who she was in relation to the house, she said, "He always came . . . every day . . . William . . . my house . . . "

"Where is he? You know where he went?"

There was anxiety in her voice now. She said he left St. Valentine's Day, this year . . . and she had no idea what year that was.

Who was Willie? Was he her husband?

This caused her to panic.

"Don't tell them!" she implored me. The story began to look ominous. Willie, Ella, the baby . . . and not her husband?

She began to cry uncontrollably now. "Willie isn't coming anymore . . . where is he?"

What was she doing in the house?

"Wait for Willie . . . by the window. . . always by the window. I wait for him and take care of Lily, she is so sweet. What I can do to find Willie?"

I began to exorcise her, seeing she could not tell me anything further about herself. Her memory was evidently limited by the ancient grief. As I did so, she began to notice spirits. "There is my Papa . . . he will be very angry . . . don't tell anyone . . . take me now . . . my Papa thinks we are married . . . but we have no marriage . . . Willie must marry me . . . "

She cried even harder now.

"Andrew . . . my husband . . . "

Once again I asked Albert, the guide, to lead her outside, from the house. It wasn't easy. It was noisy. But it worked.

"She is out," Albert reported immediately following this emotional outburst, "but her father did find out."

"What period are we in now?"

"The eighteen-something."

"Is there anything in the way of a disturbance from the more recent past?"

"Yes, that is true. An older lady . . . she does not want to give up the home."

Albert then went on to explain that the woman at the window who had been seen had actually been used in her lifetime by the earlier entities to manifest through, which created confusion in her own mind as to who she was. Albert regretted that he could not have her speak to us directly. Andrew, he explained, was that more recent woman's father. Both women died in this house, and since the earlier woman would not let go, the later woman could not go on either, Albert explained.

"We have them both on our side, but they are closer to you because their thoughts are on the earth plane, you can reach them, as you are doing."

After assuring us and the owners of the house that all was peaceful now and that the disturbed entities had been released, Albert withdrew, and Ethel returned to herself as usual blissfully ignorant of what had come through her mediumship.

Two of the ladies mentioned earlier, who had been connected with the house and the phenomena therein, had meanwhile joined us. Mrs. Anthony Brooks, a lady who had been sleeping in one of the bedrooms with her husband two years prior to our visit had this to say.

"I had been asleep, when I was awakened by ruffling at the back of my head. I first thought it was my husband and turned over. But next thing I felt was pressure on my stomach, very annoying, and I turned and realized that my husband had been sound asleep. Next, my cover was being pulled from the bed, and there was a light, a very pale light for which there was no source. I was very frightened. I went upstairs to go to the bathroom and as I was on the stairs I felt I was being pushed and held on tightly to the banister."

I next talked to Mrs. Mildred Haynes Noyes, who had been

able to identify the ghostly lady at the window as being the former resident, Mrs. Bell. Everything she had told the Brighams was being reiterated. Then Ken Brigham himself spoke, and we went over his experiences once more in greater detail.

"I was standing in front of the fireplace, painting, and at that time there was a door to that bedroom over there which has since been closed up. It was a bright morning, about eleven o'clock, the doors were open, windows were open, my wife Doris was upstairs at the time, I was alone, and as I stood there painting, I glanced out and there, standing in the doorway, *was a woman.* As I was glancing at her I thought it peculiar that the neighbors would simply walk through my house without knocking.

"She stood there simply looking at me, with her arms folded, a woman who was rather short, not too heavy, dressed in a flower-print housedress, cotton, she had on glasses and wore flat-heel Oxford shoes, all of this in plain daylight. I did not know what to say to this woman who had walked into my house. I was about to say to her, What can I do for you? thinking of nothing more to say than that, and with that — she was gone. I raced back to the hall, thinking this little old lady had moved awfully fast, but needless to say, there was no one there. I said nothing to anyone, but several weeks later, during the summer, both my wife and I were awakened several times during the night by a very chilly breeze coming into the bedroom. That was one of the bedrooms upstairs. Neither of us said anything but we both sat up in bed and as we did so, we watched a little light dance across the wall! We are very isolated here, and there is no light from the outside whatsoever. This continued for the next year."

At this point it was decided that Mrs. Brigham would tell her part of the story.

"The first summer that we had the house," Mrs. Doris Brigham began, "I was sitting here, about five in the afternoon, my husband was upstairs, and my son was outside somewhere. I was alone and I was aware that someone was here, and on this white doorway, there was a solid black shadow. It was the profile of a woman from top to bottom, I could see the sharp features, the outline of the glasses, the pug in the back of her head, the long dress and shoes — all of a sudden, the shadow disappeared, and a cold breeze came toward me, and it came around and stood in back of my chair, and all of a sudden I had this feeling of peace and contentment, and all was right with the world. Then, all of a sudden, the cold air around my chair, I could feel it moving off. Then, practically every night in the room upstairs, I was awakened for several years in the middle of the night, by a feeling of someone coming into the room. But many times there would be the dancing lights. We moved into another bedroom, but even there we would be awakened by someone running their fingers up my hair! Someone was pressing against me, and the same night, a neighbor was in the house, and she told us the same story. Footsteps of someone coming up the stairs. A feeling of movement of air. A black shadow on the ceiling, and then it disappeared. Often when the children were sick, we felt her around. It was always strong when there were children in the house."

I wondered whether she ever felt another presence in the house, apart from this woman.

Mrs. Brigham replied that one time, when she did not feel the woman around, she came into the house and felt very angry. That was someone else, she felt.

I decided it was time to verify, if possible, some of the material that had come through Mrs. Meyers in trance, and I turned to Ken Brigham for his comments.

"It has been one of the most astounding experiences I have ever had," he began. "There are several points which no one could know but my wife and myself. We did a considerable amount of research back through the deeds of the house. This only transpired a few weeks ago. I had been excavating up out front, preparing some drains, when I came across some foreign bricks, indicating that there had been an extension to the house. This is not the original house, the room we are in; there was a cottage here built for Continental soldiers, at the end of the revolutionary war.

These cottages were given to Massachusetts soldiers, in lieu of pay, and they got some acres up here. This house has been remodeled many times, the most recent around 1870. The town here was formed around 1775; the deeds we have are around 1800. Several things about the house are lost in legend. For example, down there is a brook called Mutiny Brook. There was a mutiny here, and there was bloodshed. There were Indians, yes, this was definitely Indian territory. At one time this was a very well settled area; as recently as 1900 there were houses around here."

I realized, of course, that this was no longer the case: the house we were in was totally isolated within the countryside now.

"The original town was built on this hill, but it has disappeared," Mr. Brigham continued, and then disclosed a strange coincidence (if there be such a thing!) of an actual ancestor of his having lived here generations ago, and then moving on to Canada.

"We only just discovered that at one time two brothers with their families decided to share the house and remodel it," Brigham continued his account. "But one of them died before they could move in. Much of what Mrs. Meyers spoke of in trance is known only locally."

"What about the two women Mrs. Meyers described?" I asked. "She mentioned a short, dark-haired woman."

"She was short, but had gray hair when I saw her," Mr. Brigham said. "A perfectly solid human being — I did not see her as something elusive. We only told our son about this recently, and he told us that he had heard footsteps of a man and a woman on the third floor."

"Anything else you care to comment on?"

"Well, we have the names of some of the owners over a period of time. There were many, and some of the names in the record match those given by Ethel Meyers, like Eben."

"When Mrs. Meyers mentioned the name Isabelle," Mrs. Brigham interjected, "I thought she meant to say Alice Bell, which of course was the former owner's name — the woman at the window."

"One thing I should tell you also, there seems to have been a link between the haunting and the presence of children. One of the former owners did have a child, although the neighbors never knew this," Ken Brigham said. "She had a miscarriage. Also, Lowell, Massachusetts, is where these Continental soldiers came from; that was the traditional origin at the time. Maine did not yet exist as a state; the area was still part of Massachusetts. One more thing: both Mr. and Mrs. Bell died without having any funerals performed. She died in a nursing home nearby, he in Florida. But neither had a funeral service."

"Well, they had one now," I remarked and they laughed. It was decided that the Brighams would search the records further regarding some of the other things that Ethel had said in trance, and then get back to me.

Mr. Brigham was as good as his word. On August 21, 1967, he sent me an accounting of what he had further discovered about the house, and the history of the area in which it stands. But it was not as exhaustive as I had hoped even though it confirmed many of the names and facts Ethel had given us in trance. I decided to wait until I myself could follow up on the material, when I had the chance.

Fortunately, as time passed, the Brighams came to visit my ex-wife Catherine and myself in August of the following year at our home in New York, and as a result Ken Brigham went back into the records with renewed vigor. Thus it was that on August 20, 1968, he sent me a lot of confirming material, which is presented here.

Ethel Meyers's mediumship had once again been proved right on target. The names she gave us, Bell, Eben, Murdoch, Blackguard, Willie, Abraham, why there they were in the historical records! Not ghostly fantasies, not guesswork . . . people from out of the past.

August 20, 1968

Dear Hans,

It was good hearing from Cathy and we did enjoy visiting with you. I presume that just about now you're again on one of your trips, but I promised to forward to you some additional information that we've gathered since last summer. Enclosed is a chronology of the history of the house as far as we've been able to trace back. Early this summer (the only time we made it up to Maine) we spent hours in the York, Maine, Registry of Deeds, but the trail is cold. Deeds are so vague that we can't be certain as to whether or not a particular deed refers to our property. We are, however, convinced by style of building, materials, etc., that the back part of our house is much older than thought originally — we suspect it goes back to the mid-1700s.

Although I haven't included reference to it, our reading of the town history (which is extremely garbled and not too accurate) indicates that one of the Willard boys, whose father had an adjoining farm, went off to the Civil War and never returned, although he is not listed as one of the wounded, dead, or missing. If memory serves me right, he was simply listed as W. Willard ("Willie"?). Now the "ghost" said her name was "Isabel"; unfortunately, we can find no records in the town history on the Bell family, although they owned the house from 1851 to 1959 and Eben Bell lived in the town from 1820–1900! This is peculiar in as much as nearly every other family is recounted in the Town History of 1874. Why? Could "Isabel" be a corruption of the Bell name, or perhaps there was an Isabel Bell. Checking backwards in a perpetual calendar it seems that during the mid-1800s Tuesday, St. Valentine's Day, occurred on February 14, 1865, 1860, and 1854; the first seems most logical since the others do not occur during the Civil War — which ended on [May] 26, 1865!*

Some of my other notes are self-explanatory.

Another question of course concerns the term "Blackguard" for our particular road and hill. An archaic term that connotes "rude" — note also that the map of 1850 does not show a family name beside our house . . . this could be because the property was between owners, or it could be that the owners were "rude" — which also could account for the lack of reference in Town History to the Bell family. It's an interesting sidelight.

Now, to more interesting pieces of information for you: 1) we've finally decided to sell the house and it's just like losing a child . . . I'm personally heartbroken, but I'm also a realist and it is ridiculous to try to keep it when we can't get up there often enough to maintain it. We have a couple of prospective buyers now but since we're not under pressure we want to make sure that any new owners would love it like we do and care for it.

2) And, then the strangest . . . Doris was going through some old photographs of the place and came across a color print from a slide taken by a guest we had there from Dublin, Ireland. And, it truly looks like an image in the

long view up the lane to the house. Three persons have noted this now. Then, on another slide it looks as though there were a house in the distance (also looking up the lane) which is only 1½ stories in height. We're having the company photographer blow them up to see what we will see. I'll certainly keep you posted on this!

Well, it all adds up to the fact that we did a lot more work and learned a lot more about the place . . . nearly all of which correlates with Ethel's comments. But as a Yankee realist, I'm just going to have to cast sentiment aside and let it go.

Drop us a line when you get a chance.

Sincerely yours,

*"Willie left on Tuesday, St. Valentine's Day."

Two points should be made here regarding this story. Ethel Johnson Meyers had many phases or forms of mediumship, but despite her fervent belief that she might also possess the ability to produce so-called extras, or supernormal photographs, she never did during my investigations. What she did produce at times on her own were so-called scotographs, similar to Rorschach effects used in psychiatry; they were the result of briefly exposing sensitive photographic paper to light and then interpreting the resulting shapes.

But genuine psychic photography shows clear cut images, faces, figures that need no special interpretation to be understood, and this, alas, did not occur in this case when I took the photographs with my camera in Mrs. Meyers's presence.

After the Brighams had sold the Maine property, they moved to Hampton, Virginia. Ken and Doris looked forward to many years of enjoying life in this gentler climate.

Unfortunately, exactly two years after our last contact, in August of 1970, Ken slipped and injured an ankle, which in turn led to complications and his untimely and sudden death.

As for the restless ones up in Maine, nothing further was heard, and they are presumed to be where they rightfully belong.

The following research material, supplied by the late Mr. Ken Brigham, is presented here to give the reader a better feel for the territory and times in which this took place.

Brigham's documentation:

1. Roberts, Kenneth, *March to Quebec,* Doubleday, 1938, p. 32. Listed in the King's Service: Thomas Murdock.

2. Carpenter, Allan, *Enchantment of America — Maine,* Children's Press, 1966, p. 27 — 85 years of Indian warfare, more than 1,000 Maine residents killed, hundreds captured; by year 1675, there were about 6,000 European settlers in what is now Maine.

3. Smith, Bradford, *Roger's Rangers & The French and Indian War,* Random House, 1956, p. 5 — Indians began to slaughter them when they marched out of Fort William Henry to surrender — women and children and men (1757); p. 6 — Robert Rogers of New York raised company of rangers in 1755, by 1758 had five companies. Ebenezer Webster came from his home in New Hampshire; p. 46 — mentioned Colonel Bradstreet; p. 176 — Ebenezer, 1761, returned east to Albany as Captain and then to New Hampshire where he married a girl named Mehitable Smith . . . pushed northward with men under Colonel Stevens and settled on 225 acres at northern edge of town of Salisbury. Later fought in revolutionary war.

Oxford County Registry of Deeds

(References: Book 14, p. 18; Bk. 25, p. 295; Bk. 49, p. 254; Bk.

67, p. 264; Bk. 92, p. 158; Bk. 110, p. 149; Bk. 117, p. 268; Bk. 187, p. 197; Bk. 102, p. 135; Bk. 240, p. 477–478; Bk. 260, p. 381)

1805   Abraham (or Abram) Whitney sold to Nathan Jewell
1809   Nathan Jewell sold to William Monroe (part of land and the house) (1/9/09)
1823   Jonathan Stone bankrupt and sold to Peter Gerry (house), Thaddeus Brown and Josiah Shaw (5/19/23)
1836   Peter Gerry sold to Moses M. Mason (6/14/36)
1848   John Gerry sold to Daniel Billings (5/27/48)
1895   Semantha Bell sold to Caroline Bell (3/4/95)
1940   Edna Culhan (daughter of Caroline Bell) sold to Irving and Alice Bell (11/7/40)
1956   Alice Bell transferred to Archie and Ethel Bell (10/12/56)
1959   Archie and Ethel Bell sold to K. E. and D. M. Brigham (1/59)

Bk. 3, p. 484, Feb 7, 1799

Isaac Smith of Waterford for $800 sold to Nathaniel Geary of Harvard, Lot 2 in 6th Range (southerly half). Deed written February 7, 1799, but not recorded until September 24, 1808. (m. Unice Smith) (See notes 1 & 2)

Vol. 3, p. 99, Jan 6, 1800 (Fryeburg)

Nathaniel Geary and Betey Geary, his wife, sold to Peter Geary for $400 westerly end of southern half of Lot 2 in 6th Range. Notarized in York, January 6, 1800. On April 2, 1801 Betey Geary appeared and signed document which was registered on February 11, 1804.

Peter Gerry (or Geary) b. 1776 — d. 6/16/1847
m. Mary (b. 1782 — d. 3/16/1830)
m. Elizabeth (b. 1787 — d. 5/1/1858)
    c. Mary (b. 1834 or 1804 — d. 1844)

(see note 3) John C. (b. 1808)
Roland (b. 1810 — d. 1842)
m. Maria Farrar (b. 1811 — d. 1842)
Abbie (b. 1812 — d. 1817)
Elbridge (b. 1815 — m. Anna Jenness)

Bk. 92, p. 158, May 27, 1848
John Gerry sold for $100 (?) to Daniel Billings
Daniel Billings (b. 1780 Temple, Massachusetts)
. . . m. Sarah Kimball (b. 1786)
. . . c. Louise (m. William Hamlin)
Caroline (b. 1810 — m. G. F. Wheeler — b. 1810)
George C. (b. 1837 — d. 1919)
. . . m. Rebecca Whitcomb, private F. Co., 9th Reg. — 3 years
svc. Civil War)
Maria (m. Calvin Houghton)
James R. (m. Esther Clark)
John D. (m. Esther Knowlton)
Miranda

Bk. 102, p. 135, Oct 14, 1851
Daniel Billings sold to William F. Bell of Boston and Timothy Bell
for $1,400

Bk. 117, p. 268, Dec 24, 1858
William Bell of Waterford paid his father, William F. Bell, $800 for
Lot 2 in 6th Range

Bk. 187, p. 197, April 3, 1871
William Bell, "for support of self and wife," transferred to Timothy
C. Bell "homestead farm" and its parts of lots.

Bk. 240, p. 24, 1894
Timothy Bell left property to his wife Semantha Bell

Bk. 240, p. 477–78, Mar 4, 1895

Semantha Hamlin Bell transferred to Caroline Bell of Boston
  Caroline Bell (b. 4/4/1848 — d. 9/20/1926)
  . . . m. T. C. Bell (b. 10/10/1829 — d. 7/13/1894)
  . . . m. J. B. Bennett

1905

Caroline Bell (d. 1905??) left property to her son Irving Bell, "her sole heir."

Bk. 442, p. 133, Oct 30, 1940

Edna Bell Culhan (unmarried) of Cambridge, Mass. transferred to Irving and Alice Bell

Nov. 7, 1940

Irving Bell transferred to Edna Culhan "premises described in deed from Semantha to his mother Caroline Bell and he was her sole heir."

Bk. 560, p. 381, Oct 12, 1956

Archie and Ethel Bell inherited Lot 1 & 2 in the 5th Range and Lots 1 & 2 in the 6th Range from Alice Bell

Jan 1959

Archie and Ethel Bell sold property to K. E. And D. M. Brigham

Notes

1. According to Bk. 2, pp. 445-46: On December 20, 1802, Nathaniel Gerry (wife Betey) for $800 sold to David Whitcomb of Boston, Mass., Lot 2 in 6th Range. Deed mentions road running thru land. Registered 1807 and notarized and signed by Justice of the Peace Eber Rice.

2. According to Bk. 9,. p. 467–68: On November 13, 1810, David Whitcomb for $150 sold to Peter Gerry Lot 2 in the 6th Range, including "Gerry Road." Apparently both these transactions (notes 1 & 2) were concerned with the westerly end of the northern half of Lot 2 in the 6th Range.

3. John C. Gerry (b. 1808): m. Nancy Farrar (b. 1810 — d. 1841), Nancy Sawin (b. 1819). He had an apothecary store in Fryeburg.

Interesting Notes

1. Local cemetery has gravestone of Hon. Lewis Brigham, b. 1816, d. 1866 (at Amherst, Mass.).
2. Eben Bell, (b. 8/5/1820 — d. 6/8/1900)
3. Richard and Samuel Brigham, and David Whitcomb, signed petition for incorporation on December 19, 1795.
4. Historical:

   Waterford was in York County when it applied for incorporation (January 27, 1796).

   Fryeburg (Pequawkett) was settled in 1763, Inc. 1777; in 1768 Fryeburg had population 300 plus.

   November 17, 1796 — Isaac Smith petitioned, with others, Massachusetts for incorporation. Document stated there were fifty to sixty families in "said plantation."

   History of Waterford, p. 25 — "and when the Indians attacked the growing settlements on the Androscoggin in 1781, and carried Lt. Segar* and others into Canadian captivity, Lt. Stephen Farrington led twenty-three men over this trail in hot, although vain pursuit of the savages."

   (*Lt. Nathaniel Segar had cleared a few acres in 1774. A few townships, as Waterford and New Suncook [Lovell and Sweden] had been surveyed and awaited settlers. p. 22)

   Waterford, settled 1775, incorporated 1797; population 1790 — 150; 1800 — 535

   "Spirit of 76" (Commanger/Morris, p. 605) — General Burgoyne surrenders October 1777 . . . General John Stark agreed to work with Seth Warner because Warner was from New Hampshire or the Hampshire Grants (1777).

   November 15, 1745 — First Massachusetts Regiment, under Sir

William Pepperrell — 8th company: Capt. Thomas Perkins, Lt. John Burbank, John Gerry (single).

Civil War: "Fifth Regiment commanded by Mark H. Dunnill of Portland. "Fifth was engaged in eleven pitched battles and eight skirmishes ere it entered on terrible campaign of the Wilderness which was an incessant battle. It captured 6 rebel flags and more prisoners than it had in its ranks."

5. Local Notes:

A) Androscoggin Trail was the main Indian route from the East Coast to Canada. Below our property, in the area of Lot 3 in the 4th Range, it follows a brook called "Mutiny Brook." The origin of the term used here is vague, but the natives say Indians mutinied there during the French and Indian Wars.

B) When the town was first settled, the pioneers built their homes on our hill rather than the flat land and the only road around Bear Lake was at the foot of Sweden and Blackguard roads.

C) Our road is called by the archaic word "Blackguard" which connotes villain. No one knows why.

D) The second floor of the house was constructed sometime after the first; timbers are hand hewn to the second floor and mill cut above. The house was rebuilt several times apparently; about 1890 or so two brothers and their families intended to live there but one died before taking residence. Also, foundations of an earlier building were uncovered near the back door.

The Ghost at Port Clyde

Port Clyde is a lovely little fishing village on the coast of Maine where a small number of native Yankees, who live there all year round, try to cope with a few summer residents, usually from New York or the Midwest. Their worlds do not really mesh, but the oldtimers realize that a little — not too much — tourism is really quite good for business, especially the few small hotels in and around Port Clyde and St. George, so they don't mind them too much. But the Down Easterners do keep to themselves, and it isn't always easy to get them to open up about their private lives or such things as, let us say, ghosts.

Carol Olivieri Schulte lived in Council Bluffs, Iowa, when she first contacted me in November of 1974. The wife of a lawyer, Mrs. Schulte is an inquisitive lady, a college graduate, and the mother of what was then a young son. Somehow Carol had gotten hold of some of my books and become intrigued by them, especially where ghosts were concerned, because she, too, had had a brush with the uncanny.

"It was the summer of 1972," she explained to me, "and I was sleeping in an upstairs bedroom," in the summer cottage her parents owned in Port Clyde, Maine.

"My girlfriend Marion and her boyfriend were sleeping in a bedroom across the hall with their animals, a Siamese cat and two dogs."

The cat had been restless and crept into Carol's room, touching her pillow and waking her. Carol sat up in bed, ready to turn on the light, when she saw standing beside her bed a female figure in a very white nightgown. The figure had small shoulders and long, flowing hair . . . and Carol could see right through her!

It became apparent, as she came closer, that she wanted to get Carol's attention, trying to talk with her hands.

"Her whole body suggested she was in desperate need of something. Her fingers were slender, and there was a diamond ring on her fourth finger, on the right hand. Her hands moved more desperately as I ducked under the covers."

Shortly after this, Carol had a dream contact with the same entity. This time she was abed in another room in the house, sleeping, when she saw the same young woman. She appeared to her at first in the air, smaller than life size. Her breasts were large, and there was a maternal feeling about her. With her was a small child, a boy of perhaps three years of age, also dressed in a white gown. While the child was with Carol on her bed, in the dream, the mother hovered at some distance in the corner. Carol, in the dream, had the feeling the mother had turned the child over to her, as if to protect it, and then she vanished. Immediately there followed the appearance of another woman, a black-hooded female, seeming very old, coming toward her and the child. Carol began to realize the dark-hooded woman wanted to take the child from her, and the child was afraid and clung to her. When the woman stood close to Carol's bed, still in the dream, Carol noticed her bright green eyes and crooked, large nose, and her dark complexion. She decided to fight her off, concentrating her thoughts on the white light she knew was an expression of psychic protection, and the dark-hooded woman disappeared. Carol was left with the impression that she had been connected with a school or institution of some kind. At this, the mother in her white nightgown returned and took the child back, looking at Carol with an expression of gratitude before disappearing again along with her child.

Carol woke up, but the dream was so vivid, it stayed with her for weeks, and even when she contacted me, it was still crystal clear in her mind. One more curious event transpired at the exact time Carol had overcome the evil figure in the dream. Her grandmother, whom she described as "a very reasoning, no-nonsense lively Yankee lady," had a cottage right in back of Carol's parents'. She was tending her stove, as she had done many times before, when it blew up right into her face, singing her eyebrows. There was nothing whatever wrong with the stove.

Carol had had psychic experiences before, and even her attorney husband was familiar with the world of spirits, so her contacting me for help with the house in Maine was by no means a family problem.

I was delighted to hear from her, not because a Maine ghost was so very different from the many other ghosts I had dealt with through the years, but because of the timing of Carol's request. It so happened that at that time I was in the middle of writing, producing and appearing in the NBC series called "In Search of . . ." and the ghost house in Maine would make a fine segment.

An agreement was arranged among all concerned, Carol, her husband, her parents, the broadcasting management, and me. I then set about to arrange a schedule for our visit. We had to fly into Rockland, Maine, and then drive down to Port Clyde. If I wanted to do it before Carol and her family were in residence, that, too, would be all right though she warned me about the cold climate up there during the winter months.

In the end we decided on May, when the weather would be acceptable, and the water in the house would be turned back on.

I had requested that all witnesses of actual phenomena in the house be present to be questioned by me.

Carol then sent along pictures of the house and statements from some of the witnesses. I made arrangements to have her join us at the house for the investigation and filming for the period of May 13 to 15, 1976. The team — the crew, my psychic and me — would all stay over at a local hotel. The psychic was a young woman artist named Ingrid Beckman with whom I had been working and helping develop her gift.

And so it happened that we congregated at Port Clyde from different directions, but with one purpose in mind — to contact the lady ghost at the house. As soon as we had settled in at the local hotel, the New Ocean House, we drove over to the spanking white cottage that was to be the center of our efforts for the next three days. Carol's brother Robert had driven up from Providence, and her close friend Marion Going from her home, also in Rhode Island.

I asked Ingrid to stay at a little distance from the house and wait for me to bring her inside, while I spoke to some of the witnesses out of Ingrid's earshot. Ingrid understood and sat down on the lawn, taking in the beauty of the landscape.

Carol and I walked in the opposite direction, and once again we went over her experiences as she had reported them to me in her earlier statement. But was there anything beyond that, I wondered, and questioned Carol about it.

"Now since that encounter with the ghostly lady have you seen her again? Have you ever heard her again?"

"Well about three weeks ago before I was to come out here, I really wanted to communicate with her. I concentrated on it just before I went to sleep, you know. I was thinking about it, and I dreamed that she appeared to me the way she had in the dream that followed her apparition here in this house. And then I either dreamed that I woke up momentarily and saw her right there as I had actually seen her in this bedroom or I actually did wake up and see her. Now the sphere of consciousness I was in — I am doubtful as to where I was at that point. I mean it was nothing like the experience I experienced right here in this room. I was definitely awake, and *I definitely saw that ghost.* As to this other thing a couple of weeks ago — I wasn't quite sure."

"Was there any kind of message?"

"No, not this last time."

"Do you feel she was satisfied having made contact with you?"

"Yeah, I felt that she wanted to communicate with me in the same sense that I wanted to communicate with her. Like an old friend will want to get in touch with another old friend, and I get the feeling she was just saying, 'Yes, I'm still here.'"

I then turned to Carol's brother, Bob Olivieri, and questioned him about his own encounters with anything unusual in the house. He took me to the room he was occupying at the time of the experiences, years ago, but apparently the scene was still very fresh in his mind.

"Mr. Olivieri, what exactly happened to you in this room?"

"Well, one night I was sleeping on this bed and all of a sudden I woke up and heard footsteps — what I thought were footsteps — it sounded like slippers or baby's feet in pajamas — something like that. Well, I woke up and I came over, and I stepped in this spot, and I looked in the hallway and the sound stopped. I thought maybe I was imagining it. So I came back to the bed, got into bed again, and again I heard footsteps. Well, this time I got up and as soon as I came to the same spot again and looked into the hallway it stopped. I figured it was my nephew who was still awake. So I walked down the hallway and looked into the room where my sister and nephew were sleeping, and they were both sound asleep. I checked my parents' room, and they were also asleep. I just walked back. I didn't know what to do so I got into bed again, and I kept on hearing them. I kept on walking over, and they would still be going until I stepped in this spot where they would stop. As soon as I stepped here. And this happened for an hour. I kept getting up. Heard the footsteps, stepped in this spot and they stopped. So finally I got kind of tired of it and came over to my bed and lay down in bed and as soon as I lay down I heard the steps again, exactly what happened before — and they seemed to stop at the end of the hallway. A few minutes later I felt a pressure on my sheets, starting from my feet, and going up, up, up, going up further, further, slowly but surely . . . and finally something pulled my hair! Naturally I was just scared for the rest of the night. I couldn't get to sleep."

I thought it was time to get back to Ingrid and bring her into the house. This I did, with the camera and sound people following us every step of the way to record for NBC what might transpire in the house now. Just before we entered the house, Ingrid turned to me and said, "You know that window up there? When we first arrived, I noticed someone standing in it."

"What exactly did you see?"

"It was a woman . . . and she was looking out at us."

The house turned out to be a veritable jewel of Yankee authenticity, the kind of house a sea captain might be happy in, or perhaps only a modern antiquarian. The white exterior was matched by a spanking clean, and sometimes sparse interior, with every piece of furniture of the right period — the nineteenth and early twentieth centuries — and a feeling of being lived in by many people, for many years.

After we had entered the downstairs part where there was an ample kitchen and a nice day room, I asked Ingrid, as usual, to tell me whatever psychic impression she was gathering about the house, its people and its history. Naturally, I had made sure all along that

Ingrid knew nothing of the house or the quest we had come on to Maine, and there was absolutely no way she could have had access to specifics about the area, the people in the house — past and present — nor anything at all about the case.

Immediately Ingrid set to work, she seemed agitated.

"There is a story connected here with the 1820s or the 1840s," she began, and I turned on my tape recorder to catch the impressions she received as we went along. At first, they were conscious psychic readings, later Ingrid seemed in a slight state of trance and communication with spirit entities directly. Here is what followed.

"1820s and 1840s. Do you mean both or one or the other?"

"Well, it's in that time period. And I sense a woman with a great sense of remorse."

"Do you feel this is a presence here?"

"Definitely a presence here."

"What part of the house do you feel it's strongest in?"

"Well, I'm being told to go upstairs."

"Is it a force pulling you up?"

"No, I just have a feeling to go upstairs."

"Before you go upstairs, before you came here did you have any feeling that there was something to it?"

"Yes, several weeks ago I saw a house — actually it was a much older house than this one, and it was on this site — and it was a dark house and it was shingled and it was — as I say, could have been an eighteenth century house, the house that I saw. It looked almost like a salt box, it had that particular look. And I saw that it was right on the water and I sensed a woman in it and a story concerned with a man in the sea with this house."

"A man with the sea?"

"Yes."

"Do you feel that this entity is still in the house?"

"I do, and of course I don't feel this is the *original* house. I feel it was on this property, and this is why I sense that she is throughout the house. That she comes here because this is her reenactment."

I asked her to continue.

"I can see in my mind's eye the house that was on this property before, and in my mind I sense a field back in this direction, and there was land that went with this!"

"Now we are upstairs. I want you to look into every room and give me your impressions of it," I said.

"Well, the upstairs is the most active. I sense a woman who is waiting. This is in the same time period. There are several other periods that go with this house, but I will continue with this one. I also see that she has looked out — not from this very same window, but windows in this direction of the house — *waiting for somebody to come back.*"

"What about this room?"

"Well, this room is like the room where she conducted a vigil, waiting for someone. And I just got an impression where she said that, 'She' meaning a schooner, 'was built on the Kennebec River' . . . It seems to be a double-masted schooner, and it seems to be her husband who is on this. And I have an impression of novelties that he has brought her back. Could be from a foreign country. Perhaps the Orient or something like that."

"Now go to the corridor again and try some of the other rooms. What about this one?"

"I sense a young man in this room, but this is from a different time period. It's a young boy. It seems to be 1920s."

"Is that all you sense in this room?"

"That is basically what I sense in this room. The woman of the double-masted schooner story is throughout the house because as I have said, she doesn't really belong to this house. She is basically on the *property* — mainly she still goes through this whole house looking for the man to come home. And the front of the house is where the major activity is. She is always watching. But I have an impression now of a storm that she is very upset about. A gale of some kind. It seems to be November. I also feel she is saying something about . . . flocking sheep. There are sheep on this property."

"Where would you think is the most active room?"

"The most active room I think is upstairs and to the front, where we just were. I feel it most strongly there."

"Do you think we might be able to make contact with her?"

"Yes, I think so. Definitely I feel that she is watching *and I knew about her before I came.*"

"What does she look like?"

"I see a tall woman, who is rather thin and frail with dark hair and it appears to be a white gown. It could be a nightgown I see her in — it looks like a nightgown to me with a little embroidery on the front. Hand done."

"Let us see if she cares to make contact with us?"

"All right."

"If the entity is present, and wishes to talk to us, we have come as friends; she is welcome to use this instrument, Ingrid, to manifest."

"She is very unhappy here, Hans. She says her family hailed from England. I get her name as Margaret."

"Margaret what?"

"Something like H o g e n — it begins with an H. I don't think it is Hogan, Hayden, or something like that. I'm not getting the whole name."

"What period are you in now?"

"Now she says 1843. She is very unhappy because she wanted to settle in Kennebunk; she does not like it here. She doesn't like the responsibilities of the house. Her husband liked it in this fishing village. She is very unhappy about his choice."

Ghosts of New England

"Is he from England?"

"Yes, their descendants are from England."

"You mean were they born here or in England?"

"That I'm not clear on. But they have told me that their descendants are English."

"Now is she here . . . ?"

"She calls Kennebunk the city. That to her is a center."

"What does she want? Why is she still here?"

"She's left with all this responsibility. Her husband went on a ship, to come back in two years."

"Did he?"

"No, she's still waiting for him."

"The name of the ship?"

"I think it's St. Catherine."

"Is it his ship? Is he a captain?"

"He is second in command. It's not a mate, but a second something or other."

"What is she looking for?"

"She's looking to be relieved."

"Of what?"

"Of the duties and the responsibilities."

"For what?"

"This house."

"Is she aware of her passing?"

"No, she's very concerned over the flocks. She says it's now come April, and it's time for shearing. She is very unhappy over this. In this direction, Hans, I can see what appears to be a barn, and it's very old fashioned. She had two cows."

"Is she aware of the people in the house now?"

"She wants to communicate."

"What does she want them to do for her?"

"She wants for them to help her with the farm. She says it's too much, and the soil is all rocky and she can't get labor from the town. She's having a terrible time. It's too sandy here."

"Are there any children? Is she alone?"

"They have gone off, she says."

"And she's alone now?"

"Yes, she is."

"Can you see her?"

"Yes, I do see her."

"Can she see you?"

"Yes."

"Tell her that this is 1976, and that much time has passed. Does she understand this?"

"She just keeps complaining; she has nobody to write letters to."

"Does she understand that her husband has passed on and that she herself is a spirit and that there is no need to stay if she doesn't wish to?"

"She needs to get some women from the town to help with the spinning."

"Tell her that the new people in the house are taking care of everything, and she is relieved and may go on. She's free to go."

"She said, 'to Kennebunk?'"

"Any place she wishes — to the city or to join her husband on the other side of life."

"She said, 'Oh, what I would do for a town house.'"

"Ask her to call out to her husband to take her away. He's waiting for her."

"What does Johnsbury mean? A Johnsbury."

"It's a place."

"She asking about Johnsbury."

"Does she wish to go there?"

"She feels someone may be there who could help her."

Ghosts of New England

"Who?"

"It seems to be an uncle in Johnsbury."

"Then tell her to call out to her uncle in Johnsbury."

"She says he has not answered her letters."

"But if she speaks up now he will come for her. Tell her to do it now. Tell Margaret we are sending her to her uncle, with our love and compassion. That she need not stay here any longer. That she need not wait any longer for someone who cannot return. That she must go on to the greater world that awaits her outside, where she will rejoin her husband and she can see her uncle."

"She is wanting to turn on the lights. She is talking about the oil lamps. She wants them all lit."

"Tell her the people here will take good care of the house, of the lamps, and of the land."

"And she is saying, no tallow for the kitchen."

"Tell her not to worry."

"And the root cellar is empty."

"Tell her not to worry. We will take care of that for her. She is free to go — she is being awaited, she is being expected. Tell her to go on and go on from here in peace and with our love and compassion."

"She is looking for a lighthouse, or something about a lighthouse that disturbs her."

"What is the lighthouse?"

"She is very upset. She doesn't feel that it's been well kept; that this is one of the problems in this area. No one to tend things. I ought to be in Kennebunk, she says, where it is a city."

"Who lives in Kennebunk that she knows?"

"No one she knows. She wants to go there."

"What will she do there?"

"Have a town house."

"Very well, then let her go to Kennebunk."

"And go [to] the grocer," she says.

"Tell her she's free to go to Kennebunk. That we will send her there if she wishes. Does she wish to go to Kennebunk?"

"Yes, she does."

"Then tell her — tell her we are sending her now. With all our love . . . "

"In a carriage?"

"In a carriage."

"A black carriage with two horses."

"Very well. Is she ready to go?"

"Oh, I see her now in a fancy dress with a bonnet. But she's looking younger — she's looking much younger now. And I see a carriage out front with two dark horses and a man with a hat ready to take her."

"Did she get married in Kennebunk?"

"No."

"Where did she get married?"

"I don't get that."

"Is she ready to go?"

"Yes, she is."

"Tell her to get into the carriage and drive off."

"Yes, she's ready."

"Then go, Margaret — go."

"She says, many miles — three-day trip."

"All right. Go with our blessings. Do you see her in the carriage now?"

"Yes, the road goes this way. She is going down a winding road."

"Is she alone in the carriage?"

"Yes, she is, but there is a man driving."

"Who is the man who is driving?"

"A hired man."

"Is she in the carriage now?"

"Yes, she is."

"Is she on her way?"

"Yes."

"All right, then wave at her and tell her we send her away with our love."

"She looks to be about 22 now. Much younger."

"She's not to return to this house."

"She doesn't want to. She grew old in this house, she says."

"What was the house called then?"

"It was Point something."

"Did they build the house? She and her husband?"

"No, it was there."

"Who built it?"

"Samuel."

"And who was Samuel?"

"A farmer."

"They bought it from him?"

"Yes, they did. She says the deed is in the town hall."

"Of which town? Is it in this village?"

"Next town. Down the road."

"I understand. And in whose name is the deed?"

"Her husband's."

"First name."

"James."

"James what. Full name."

"It's something like Haydon."

"James Haydon from . . . ? What is Samuel's first name?"

"Samuels was the last name of the people who owned it."

"But the first name of the man who sold it. Does she remember that?"

"She never knew it."

"In what year was that?"

"1821."

"How much did they pay for the house?"

"Barter."

"What did they give them?"

"A sailing ship. A small sailing ship for fishing, and several horses. A year's supply of roots, and some paper — currency. Notes."

"But no money?"

"Just notes. Like promises, she says. Notes of promises."

"What was the full price of the house?"

"All in barter, all in exchange up here."

"But there was no sum mentioned for the house? No value?"

"She says, 'Ask my husband.'"

"Now did she and her husband live here alone?"

"Two children."

"What were their names?"

"Philip. But he went to sea."

"And the other one?"

"Francis."

"Did he go to sea too?"

"No."

"What happened to him?"

"I think Francis died."

"What did he die of?"

"Cholera. He was 17."

"Where did they get married? In what church?"

"Lutheran."

"Why Lutheran? Was she Lutheran?"

"She doesn't remember."

"Does she remember the name of the minister?"

"Thorpe."

Ghosts of New England

"Thorpe?"

"Yes. Thorpe."

"What was his first name?"

"Thomas Thorpe."

"And when they were married, was that in this town?"

"No."

"What town was it in?"

"A long way away."

"What was the name of the town?"

"Something like Pickwick . . . a funny name like that . . . it's some kind of a province of a place. A Piccadilly — a province in the country she says."

"And they came right here after that? Or did they go anywhere else to live?"

"Saco. They went into Saco."

"That's the name of a place?"

"Yes."

"How long did they stay there?"

"Six months in Saco."

"And then?"

"Her husband had a commission."

"What kind of commission?"

"On a whaling ship."

"What was the name of the ship?"

"*St. Catherine.* I see *St. Catherine* or *St. Catherines.*"

"And then where did they move to?"

"Port Clyde."

" . . . and they stayed here for the rest of their lives?"

"Yes, until he went to sea and didn't come back one time."

"His ship didn't come back?"

"No."

"Does she feel better for having told us this?"

"Oh, yes."

"Tell her that she . . . "

"She says it's a long story."

"Tell her that she need not stay where so much unhappiness has transpired in her life. Tell her her husband is over there . . . "

"Yes."

"Does she understand?"

"Yes, she does."

"Does she want to see him again?"

"Yes."

"Then she must call out to him to come to her. Does she understand that?"

"Yes."

"Then tell her to call out to her husband James right now."

"He'll take her to Surrey or something like that, he says."

"Surrey."

"Surrey. Some funny name."

"Is it a place?"

"Yes, it is."

"Does she see him?"

"Yes."

"Are they going off together?"

"Yes, I see her leaving, slowly, but she's looking back."

"Tell her to go and not to return here. Tell her to go with love and happiness and in peace. Are they gone?"

"They are going. It's a reunion."

"We wish them well and we send them from this house, with our blessings, with our love and compassion, and in peace. Go on, go on. What do you see?"

"They are gone."

And with that, we left the house, having done enough for one day, a very full day. The camera crew packed up, so that we could continue shooting in the morning. As for me, the real work was yet to come: corroborating the material Ingrid Beckman had come up with.

I turned to Carol for verification, if possible, of some of the names and data Ingrid had come up with while in the house. Carol showed us a book containing maps of the area, and we started to check it out.

"Look," Carol said and pointed at the passage in the book, "this strip of land was owned by John Barter and it was right next to Samuel Gardner . . . and it says John Barter died in 1820 . . . the date mentioned by Ingrid! Ah, and there is also mention of the same Margaret Barter, and there is a date on the same page, November 23, 1882 . . . I guess that is when she died."

"Great," I said, pleased to get all this verification so relatively easily. "What exactly is this book?"

"It's a copy of the town's early records, the old hypothogue, of the town of St. George."

"Isn't that the town right next door?"

"Yes, it is."

"What about the name Hogden or Hayden or Samuel?"

"Samuel Hatton was a sailor and his wife was named Elmira," Carol said, pointing at the book. Ingrid had joined us now as I saw no further need to keep her in the dark regarding verifications — her part of the work was done.

"We must verify that," I said. "Also, was there ever a ship named *St. Catherine* and was it built on the Kennebec River as Ingrid claimed?"

But who would be able to do that? Happily, fate was kind; there was a great expert who knew both the area and history of the towns better than anyone around, and he agreed to receive us. That turned out to be a colorful ex-sailor by the name of Commander Albert Smalley, who received us in his house in St. George — a house, I might add, which was superbly furnished to suggest the bridge of a ship. After we had stopped admiring his mementos, and made some chitchat to establish the seriousness of our mission, I turned to the Commander and put the vital questions to him directly.

"Commander Albert Smalley, you've been a resident in this town for how long?"

"I was born in this town seventy-six years ago."

"I understand you know more about the history of Port Clyde than anybody else."

"Well, that's a moot question, but I will say, possibly, yes."

"Now, to the best of your knowledge, do the names Samuel and Hatton mean anything in connection with this area?"

"Yes, I know Hatton lived at Port Clyde prior to 1850. That I'm sure about."

"What profession did he have?"

"Sailor."

"Was there a ship named the *St. Catherine* in these parts?"

"Yes, there was."

"And would it have been built at the Kennebec River? Or connected with it in some way?"

"Well, as I recall it was, and I believe it was built in the Sewell Yard at the Kennebec River."

"Was there any farming in a small way in the Port Clyde area in the nineteenth century?"

"Oh yes, primarily that's what they came here for. But fishing, of course, was a prime industry."

"Now there's a lighthouse not far from Port Clyde which I believe was built in the early part of the nineteenth century. Could it have been there in the 1840s?"

"Yes. It was built in 1833."

"Now if somebody would have been alive in 1840, would they somehow be concerned about this comparatively new lighthouse?

Would it have worried them?"

"No, it would not. The residence is comparatively new. The old stone residence was destroyed by lightning. But the tower is the same one."

"Now you know the area of Port Clyde where the Leah Davis house now stands? Prior to this house, were there any houses in the immediate area?"

"I've always been told that there was a house there. The Davis that owned it told me that he built on an old cellar."

"And how far back would that go?"

"That would go back to probably 1870. The new house was built around 1870."

"And was there one before that?"

"Yes, there was one before that."

"Could that have been a farmhouse?"

"Yes, it could have been because there is a little farm in back of it. It's small."

"Now you of course have heard all kinds of stories — some of them true, some of them legendary. Have you ever heard any story of a great tragedy concerning the owners of the farmhouse on that point?"

"Whit Thompson used to tell some weird ghost stories. But everyone called him a damned liar. Whether it's true or not, I don't know, but I've heard them."

"About that area?"

"About that area."

"Was there, sir, any story about a female ghost — a woman?"

"I have heard of a female ghost. Yes, Whit used to tell that story."

"What did he tell you?"

"That was a long time ago, and I cannot recall just what he said about it—he said many things — but she used to appear, especially on foggy nights, and it was hard to distinguish her features — that was one of the things he used to tell about — and there was something about her ringing the bell at the lighthouse, when they used to ring the old fog bell there. I don't recall what it was."

"Now the story we found involved a woman wearing a kind of white gown, looking out to sea from the window as if she were expecting her sailor to return, and she apparently was quite faceless at first."

"I don't think Whitney ever told of her face being seen."

"Do you know of anybody in your recollection who has actually had an unusual experience in that particular area?"

"No, I don't."

"Commander, if you had the choice of spending the night in the house in question, would it worry you?"

"No, why should it?"

"You are not afraid of ghosts?"

"No. Why should I be?"

"They are people after all."

"Huh?"

"They are just people after all."

"Yes."

"Have you ever seen one?"

"No, I was brought up with mediums and spiritualists and as a kid I was frightened half to death, I didn't dare go out after dark, but I got over that."

"Thank you very much."

"The lighthouse and the gale . . . the ship in a gale . . . it all seems to fit . . . , " Ingrid mumbled as we got back into our cars and left the Commander's house.

And there you have it. A girl from the big city who knows nothing about the case I am investigating, nor where she might be taken, and still comes up with names and data she could not possibly know on her own. Ingrid Beckman was (and is, I suppose) a gifted psychic. Shortly after we finished taping the Port Clyde story, I left for Europe.

While I was away, Ingrid met a former disc jockey then getting interested in the kind of work she and I had been doing so successfully for a while. Somehow he persuaded her to give a newspaper interview about this case — which, of course, upset NBC a lot since this segment would not air for six months — not to mention myself. The newspaper story was rather colorful, making it appear that Ingrid had heard of this ghost and taken care of it . . . but then newspaper stories sometimes distort things, or perhaps the verification and research of a ghost story is less interesting to them than the story itself. But to a professional like myself, the evidence only becomes evidence when it is carefully verified. I haven't worked with Ingrid since.

As for the ghostly lady of Port Clyde, nothing further has been heard about her, either, and since we gently persuaded her not to hang on any longer, chances are indeed that she has long been joined by her man, sailing an ocean where neither gales nor nosy television crews can intrude.

Haunted Is the Trailer

Sometimes, one would think, the work of a psychic investigator must be downright drab. Little old ladies have nightmares, imaginative teenagers let off steam over frustrations in directions as yet unexplored, neurotics of uncertain sexuality fantasize about their special roles and talents. All this is grist for the investigator's mill, poor chap, and he has to listen and nod politely, for that's how he gets information. (The question Peter Lorre whispered across the screen, "Where is the information?" is the beacon toward which the psychic sleuth must be drawn.) And in fact it is perfectly possible for such people to have genuine ESP experiences. Anybody can play this game. All he or she needs is to be alive and kicking. ESP comes to just about everyone, and there's nothing anyone can do about it one way or the other. It is, therefore, necessary to have a completely open mind as to the kind of individual who might have a valid psychic experience. I can attest to this need much to my regret.

Several years ago, people approached me who had witnessed the amazing Ted Serios demonstrate his thought photography and who wanted me to work with the fellow. But my quasi-middle-class sense of propriety shied away from the midwestern bellhop when I realized that he drank and was not altogether of drawing room class. How wrong I was! A little later, Professor Jules Eisenbud of the University of Colorado showed better sense and less prejudice as to a person's private habits, and his work with Serios is not only a scientific breakthrough of the first order but was turned into a successful book for Eisenbud as well.

So it was with more than casual interest that I received a communication (via the U.S. mail) from a comely young lady named Rita Atlanta.

Her initial letter merely requested that I help her get rid of her ghost. Such requests are not unusual, but this one was — and I am not referring to the lady's occupation — exotic dancing in sundry nightclubs around the more or less civilized world. What made her case unusual was the fact that her ghost appeared in a thirty-year-old trailer near Boston.

"When I told my husband that we had a ghost," she wrote, "he laughed and said, 'Why should a respectable ghost move into a trailer? We have hardly room in it ourselves with three kids.'"

* * *

It seemed the whole business had started during the summer when the specter made its first sudden appearance. Although her husband could not see what she saw, Miss Atlanta's pet skunk evidently didn't like it and moved into another room. Three months later, her husband passed away, and Miss Atlanta was kept busy hopping the Atlantic (hence her stage name) in quest of nightclub work.

Since her first encounter with the figure of a man in her Massachusetts trailer, the dancer had kept the lights burning all night long. As someone once put it, "I don't believe in ghosts, but I'm scared of them."

Despite the lights, Miss Atlanta always felt a presence at the same time that her initial experience had taken place — between three and three-thirty in the morning. It would awaken her with such regularity that at last she decided to seek help.

At the time she contacted me, she was appearing nightly at the Imperial in Frankfurt, Germany, taking a bath onstage in an oversized champagne glass filled with under-quality champagne. The discriminating clientele that frequents the Imperial loved the French touch, and Rita Atlanta was and is a wow.

I discovered that her late husband was Colonel Frank Bane, an air force ace who had originally encouraged the Vienna-born girl to change from ballet to belly dancing, and eventually to what is termed exotic dancing, but which is better described as stripping.

I decided to talk to the "Champagne Bubble Girl" on my next overseas trip. She was working at that time in Stuttgart, but she came over to meet us at our Frankfurt hotel, and my wife was immediately taken with her pleasant charm and lack of show business phoniness. Then it was discovered that Rita was a Libra, like Catherine, and we repaired for lunch to the terrace of a nearby restaurant to discuss the ups and downs of a hectic life in a champagne glass, not forgetting the three kids in a house trailer.

* * *

In September of the previous year, she and her family had moved into a brand new trailer in Peabody, Massachusetts. After her encounter with the ghost, Rita made some inquiries about the nice grassy spot where she had chosen to park the trailer. Nothing had ever stood on the spot before. No ghost stories. Nothing. Just one little thing.

One of the neighbors in the trailer camp, which is at the outskirts of greater Boston, came to see her one evening. By this time Rita's heart was already filled with fear, fear of the unknown that had suddenly come into her life here. She freely confided in her neighbor, a girl by the name of Birdie Gleason. To her amazement, the neighbor nodded with understanding. She, too, had felt "something," an unseen presence in her house trailer next to Rita's.

"Sometimes I feel someone is touching me," she told Rita.

"What exactly did *you* see?" I asked Rita. Outside the street noises of Frankfurt belied the terrifying subject we were discussing.

"I saw a big man, almost seven foot tall, about three hundred fifty pounds, and he wore a long coat and a big hat."

But the ghost didn't just stand there glaring at her. Sometimes he made himself comfortable on her kitchen counter, with his ghostly legs dangling down from it. He was as solid as a man of flesh and blood, except that she could not see his face clearly since it was in the darkness of early morning.

Later, when I visited the house trailer with my highly sensitive camera, I took some pictures in the areas indicated by Miss Atlanta: the bedroom, the door to it, and the kitchen counter. In all three areas, strange phenomena manifested on my film. Some mirrorlike transparencies developed in normally opaque areas, which could not and cannot be explained.

When it happened the first time, she raced for the light and turned the switch, her heart beating wildly. The yellowish light of the electric lamp bathed the bedroom in a nightmarish twilight. But the spook had vanished. There was no possible way a real intruder could have come and gone so fast. No way out, no way in. Because this was during the time Boston was being terrorized by the infamous Boston Strangler, Rita had taken special care to double-lock the doors and secure all the windows. Nobody could have entered the trailer without making a great deal of noise. I have examined the locks and the windows — not even Houdini could have done it.

The ghost, having once established himself in Rita's bedroom, returned for additional visits — always in the early morning hours.

Sometimes he appeared three times a week, sometimes more often.

"He was staring in my direction all the time," Rita said with a slight Viennese accent. One could see that the terror had never really left her eyes. Even three thousand miles away, the spectral stranger had a hold on the woman.

Was he perhaps looking for something? No, he didn't seem to be. In the kitchen, he either stood by the table or sat down on the counter. Ghosts don't need food — so why the kitchen?

"Did he ever take his hat off?" I asked.

"No, never," she said and smiled. Imagine a ghost doffing his hat to the lady of the trailer!

What was particularly horrifying was the noiselessness of the apparition. She never heard any footfalls or rustling of his clothes as he silently passed by. There was no clearing of the throat as if he wanted to speak. Nothing. Just silent stares. When the visitations grew more frequent, Rita decided to leave the lights on all night. After that, she did not *see* him anymore. But he was still there, at the usual hour, standing behind the bed, staring at her. She knew he was. She could almost feel the sting of his gaze.

One night she decided she had been paying huge light bills long enough. She hopped out of bed, turned the light switch off and, as the room was plunged back into semidarkness, she lay down in bed again. Within a few minutes her eyes had gotten accustomed to the dark. Her senses were on the alert, for she was not at all sure what she might see. Finally, she forced herself to turn her head in the direction of the door. Was her mind playing tricks on her? There, in the doorway, stood the ghost — as big and brooding as ever.

With a scream, she dove under the covers. When she came up, eternities later, the shadow was gone from the door.

The next evening, the lights were burning again in the trailer, and every night thereafter, until it was time for her to fly to Germany for her season's nightclub work. Then she closed up the trailer, sent her children to stay with friends, and left with the faint hope that on her return in the winter, the trailer might be free of its ghost. But she wasn't at all certain.

It was getting dark outside now, and I knew Miss Atlanta soon had to fly back to Stuttgart for her evening's work. It was obvious to me that this exotic dancer was a medium, as only the psychic can see apparitions. I queried her about the past, and reluctantly she talked of her early years in Austria.

* * *

When she was a schoolgirl of eight, she suddenly felt herself compelled to draw a picture of a funeral. Her father was puzzled by the choice of so somber a subject by a little girl. But as she pointed out who the figures in her drawing were, ranging from her father to the more distant relatives, her father listened with lips tightly drawn. When the enumeration was over, he inquired in a voice of incredulity mixed with fear, "But who is being buried?"

"Mother," the little girl replied, without a moment's hesitation, and no more was said about it.

Three weeks later to the day, her mother was dead.

The war years were hard on the family. Her father, a postal employee, had a gift for playing the numbers, allegedly on advice from his deceased spouse. But Germany's invasion ended all that and eventually Rita found herself in the United States and married to an air force colonel.

She had forgotten her psychic experiences of the past, when the ghost in the trailer brought them all back only too vividly. She was frankly scared, knowing her abilities to receive messages from the beyond. But who was this man?

* * *

I visited Peabody with a medium to see what we could learn. Rita's oldest son greeted us at the door. It wasn't until the winter of the same year that Rita showed me around her trailer. It was a cold and moist afternoon.

Her son had seen nothing and neither believed nor disbelieved his mother. But he was willing to do some legwork for me to find out who the shadowy visitor might be.

It was thus that we learned that a few years before a man had been run over by a car very close by. Had the dead man, confused about his status, sought refuge in the trailer — the nearest house in his path? Was he trying to make contact with what he could sense was a medium, who would be able to receive his anxious pleas?

It was at this time that I took the unusual photographs of the areas Rita pointed out as being haunted. Several of these pictures show unusual mirrorlike areas, in which something must have been present in the atmosphere. But the ghost did not appear for me or, for that matter, Rita. And he has not reappeared since.

Perhaps our discovery of his problem and our long and passionate discussion of the situation reached his spectral consciousness, and he knew that he was out of his element in a trailer belonging to people not connected with his world.

Was this his way of finally, belatedly, doffing his hat to the lady of the house trailer, with an apology for his intrusions?

I haven't had any further word from Rita Atlanta, but the newspapers carry oversize ads now and then telling some city of the sensational performance of the girl in the champagne glass.

It is safe to assume that she can take her bath in the glass completely alone, something she had not been sure of before. For Rita, the eyes of a couple hundred visiting firemen in a Frankfurt nightclub are far less bothersome than one solitary pair of eyes staring from another world.

Ghosts around Boston

Sometime back, I often went to Boston to appear on radio or television, and as a result people kept telling me of their own psychic adventures — and problems. I tried to follow up on as many of these cases as I could, but there are limits even to my enthusiasm.

Since having a ghostly experience is not necessarily what people like to advertise — especially to the neighbors — some of these stories, which are all true, contain only the initials of the people involved. I, of course, know them but have promised not to divulge their full names, or heaven forbid, exact addresses.

* * *

Mrs. Geraldine W. is a graduate of Boston City Hospital and works as a registered nurse; her husband is a teacher, and they have four children. Neither Mr. nor Mrs. W. ever had the slightest interest in the occult; in fact, Mrs. W. remembers hearing some chilling stories about ghosts as a child and considering them just so many fairy tales.

One July, the W.'s decided to acquire a house about twenty

miles from Boston, as the conditions in the city seemed inappropriate for bringing up their four children. They chose a Victorian home sitting on a large rock overlooking a golf course in a small town.

Actually, there are two houses built next door to each other by two brothers. The one to the left had originally been used as a winter residence, while the other, their choice, was used as a summer home. It was a remarkable sight, high above the other houses in the area. The house so impressed the W.'s that they immediately expressed their interest in buying it. They were told that it had once formed part of the H. estate, and had remained in the same family until nine years prior to their visit. Originally built by a certain Ephraim Hamblin, it had been sold to the H. family and remained a family property until it passed into the hands of the P. family. It remained in the P.'s possession until the W.'s acquired it that spring.

Prior to obtaining possession of the house, Mrs. W. had a strange dream in which she saw herself standing in the driveway, looking up at the house. In the dream she had a terrible feeling of foreboding, as if something dreadful had happened in the house. On awakening the next morning, however, she thought no more about it and later put it out of her mind.

Shortly after they moved in on July 15, Mrs. W. awoke in the middle of the night for some reason. She looked up to the ceiling and saw what looked to her like a sparkler. It swirled about in a circular movement, then disappeared. On checking, Mrs. W. found that all the shades were drawn in the room, so it perplexed her how such a light could have appeared on the ceiling. But the matter quickly slipped from her mind.

Several days later, she happened to be sitting in the livingroom one evening with the television on very low since her husband was asleep on the couch. Everything was very quiet. On the arm of a wide-armed couch there were three packages of cigarettes side by side. As she looked at them, the middle package suddenly flipped over by itself and fell to the floor. Since Mrs. W. had no interest in psychic phenomena, she dismissed this as probably due to some natural cause. A short time thereafter, she happened to be sleeping in her daughter's room, facing directly alongside the front hall staircase. The large hall light was burning since the lamp near the children's rooms had burned out. As she lay in the room, she became aware of heavy, slow, plodding footsteps coming across the hallway.

Terrified, she kept her eyes closed tight because she thought there was a prowler in the house. Since everyone was accounted for, only a stranger could have made the noises. She started to pray over and over in order to calm herself, but the footsteps continued on the stairs, progressing down the staircase and around into the livingroom where they faded away. Mrs. W. was thankful that her prayers had been answered and that the prowler had left.

Just as she started to doze off again the footsteps returned. Although she was still scared, she decided to brave the intruder, whoever he might be. As she got up and approached the area where she heard the steps, they resounded directly in front of her — yet she could see absolutely no one. The next morning she checked all the doors and windows and found them securely locked, just as she had left them the night before. She mentioned the matter to her husband, who ascribed it to nerves. A few nights later, Mrs. W. was again awakened in the middle of the night, this time in her own bedroom. As she woke and sat up in bed, she heard a woman's voice from somewhere in the room. It tried to form words, but Mrs. W. could not make them out. The voice was hollow and sounded like something from an echo chamber. It seemed to her that the voice had come from an area near the ceiling over her husband's bureau. The incident did not prevent her from going back to sleep, perplexing though it was.

By now Mrs. W. was convinced that they had a ghost in the house. She was standing in her kitchen, contemplating where she could find a priest to have the house exorcised, when all of a sudden a trash bag, which had been resting quietly on the floor, burst open, spilling its contents all over the floor. The disturbances had become so frequent that Mrs. W. took every opportunity possible to leave the house early in the morning with her children, and not go home until she had to. She did not bring in a priest to exorcise the house, but managed to obtain a bottle of blessed water from Lourdes. She went through each room, sprinkling it and praying for the soul of whoever was haunting the house.

One evening, Mr. W. came home from work around six o'clock and went upstairs to change his clothes while Mrs. W. was busy setting the table for dinner. Suddenly Mr. W. called his wife and asked her to open and close the door to the back hall stairs. Puzzled by his request, she did so five times, each time more strenuously. Finally she asked her husband the purpose of this exercise. He admitted that he wanted to test the effect of the door being opened and closed in this manner because he had just observed the back gate to the stairs opening and closing by itself!

This was as good a time as any to have a discussion of what was going on in the house, so Mrs. W. went upstairs to join Mr. W. in the bedroom where he was standing. As she did so, her eye caught a dim, circular light that seemed to skip across the ceiling in two strokes; at the same time, the shade at the other end of the room suddenly snapped up, flipping over vigorously a number of times. Both Mr. and Mrs. W. started to run from the room; then, catching themselves, they returned to the bedroom.

On looking over these strange incidents, Mrs. W. admitted that there had been some occurrences that could not be explained by natural means. Shortly after they had moved to the house, Mr. W. had started to paint the interior, at the same time thinking about making some structural changes in the house because there were certain things in it he did not like. As he did so, two cans of paint were knocked out of his hands, flipping over and covering a good portion of the livingroom and hall floors.

Then there was that Saturday afternoon when Mr. W. had helped his wife vacuum the hall stairs. Again he started to talk about the bad shape the house was in, in his opinion, and as he condemned the house, the vacuum cleaner suddenly left the upper landing and traveled over the staircase all by itself, finally hitting him on the head with a solid thud!

But their discussion did not solve the matter; they had to brace themselves against further incidents, even though they did not know why they were happening or who caused them.

One evening Mrs. W. was feeding her baby in the livingroom near the fireplace, when she heard footsteps overhead and the dragging of something very heavy across the floor. This was followed by a crashing sound on the staircase, as if something very heavy had fallen against the railing. Her husband was asleep, but Mrs. W. woke him up and together they investigated, only to find the children asleep and no stranger in the house.

It was now virtually impossible to spend a quiet evening in the livingroom without hearing some uncanny noise. There was scratching along the tops of the doors inside the house, a rubbing sound along the door tops, and once in a while the front doorknob would turn by itself, as if an unseen hand were twisting it. No one could have done this physically because the enclosed porch leading to the door was locked and the locks were intact when Mrs. W. examined them.

The ghost, whoever he or she was, roamed the entire house. One night Mrs. W. was reading in her bedroom at around midnight when she heard a knocking sound halfway up the wall of her room. It seemed to move along the wall and then stop dead beside her night table. Needless to say, it did not contribute to a peaceful night. By now the older children were also aware of the disturbances. They, too, heard knocking on doors with no one outside, and twice Mrs. W.'s little girl, then seven years old, was awakened in the middle of the night because she heard someone walking about the house. Both her parents were fast asleep.

That year, coming home on Christmas night to an empty house, or what they *presumed* to be an empty house, the W.'s noticed that a Christmas light was on in the bedroom window. Under the circumstances, the family stayed outside while Mr. W. went upstairs to check the house. He found everything locked and no one inside. The rest of the family then moved into the lower hall, waiting for Mr. W. to come down from upstairs. As he reached the bottom of the stairs, coming from what he assured his family was an empty upper story, they all heard footsteps overhead from the area he had just examined.

On the eve of St. Valentine's Day, Mrs. W. was readying the house for a party the next evening. She had waxed the floors and spruced up the entire house, and it had gotten late. Just before going to bed, she decided to sit down for a while in her rocking chair. Suddenly she perceived a moaning and groaning sound coming across the livingroom from left to right. It lasted perhaps ten to fifteen seconds, then ended as abruptly as it had begun.

During the party the next evening, the conversation drifted to ghosts, and somehow Mrs. W. confided in her sister-in-law about what they had been through since moving to the house. It was only then that Mrs. W. found out from her sister-in-law that her husband's mother had had an experience in the house while staying over one night during the summer. She, too, had heard loud footsteps coming up the hall stairs; she had heard voices, and a crackling sound as if there had been a fire someplace. On investigating these strange noises, she had found nothing that could have caused them. However, she had decided not to tell Mrs. W. about it, in order not to frighten her.

Because of her background and position, and since her husband was a respected teacher, Mrs. W. was reluctant to discuss their experiences with anyone who might construe them as imaginary, or think the family silly. Eventually, however, a sympathetic neighbor gave her one of my books, and Mrs. W. contacted me for advice. She realized, of course, that her letter would not be read immediately, and that in any event, I might not be able to do anything about it for some time. Frightening though the experiences had been, she was reconciled to living with them, hoping only that her children would not be hurt or frightened.

On March 3, she had put her three young boys to bed for a nap and decided to check if they were properly covered. As she went up the stairway, she thought she saw movement out of the corner of her eye. Her first thought was that her little boy, then four years old, had gotten up instead of taking his nap. But, on checking, she found him fast asleep.

Exactly one week later, Mrs. W. was in bed trying to go to sleep when she heard a progressively louder tapping on the wooden mantle at the foot of the bed. She turned over to see where the noise was coming from or what was causing it when it immediately stopped. She turned back to the side, trying to go back to sleep, when suddenly she felt something or someone shake her foot as though trying to get her attention. She looked down at her foot and saw absolutely nothing.

Finally, on March 26, she received my letter explaining some of the phenomena to her and advising her what to do. As she was reading my letter, she heard the sound of someone moving about upstairs, directly over her head. Since she knew that the children were sleeping soundly, Mrs. W. realized that her unseen visitor was not in the least bit put off by the advice dispensed her by the ghost hunter. Even a dog the W.'s had acquired around Christmas had its difficulty with the unseen forces loose in the house.

At first, he had slept upstairs on the rug beside Mrs. W.'s bed. But a short time after, he began to growl and bark at night, especially in the direction of the stairs. Eventually he took to sleeping on the enclosed porch and refused to enter the house, no matter how one would try to entice him. Mrs. W. decided to make some inquiries in the neighborhood, in order to find out who the ghost might be or what he might want.

She discovered that a paper-hanger who had come to do some work in the house just before they had purchased it had encountered considerable difficulties. He had been hired to do some paper hanging in the house, changing the decor from what it had been. He had papered a room in the house as he had been told to, but on returning the next day found that some of his papers were on upside down, as if moved around by unseen hands. He, too, heard strange noises and would have nothing further to do with the house. Mrs. W. then called upon the people who had preceded them in the house, the P. family, but the daughter of the late owner said that during their stay in the house they had not experienced anything unusual. Perhaps she did not care to discuss such matters. At any rate, Mrs. W. discovered that the former owner, Mr. P., had actually died in the house three years prior to their acquisition of it. Apparently, he had been working on the house, which he loved very much, and had sustained a fracture. He recovered from it, but sustained another fracture in the same area of his leg. During the recovery, he died of a heart attack in the livingroom.

It is conceivable that Mr. P. did not like the rearrangements made by the new owners and resented the need for repapering or repainting, having done so much of that himself while in the flesh. But if it is he who is walking up and down the stairs at night, turning doorknobs, and appearing as luminous balls of light — who, then, is the woman whose voice has also been heard?

So it appears that the house overlooking the golf course for the past hundred and twenty-two years has more than one spectral inhabitant in it. Perhaps Mr. P. is only a johnny-come-lately, joining the earlier shades staying on in what used to be their home. As far as the W.'s are concerned, the house is big enough for all of them, so long as they know their place!

*   *   *

Peter Q. comes from a devout Catholic family, part Scottish, part Irish. One June, Peter Q. was married, and his brother Tom, with whom he had always maintained a close and cordial relationship, came to the wedding. That was the last time the two brothers were happy together.

Two weeks later Tom and a friend spent a weekend on Cape Cod. During that weekend, Tom lost his prize possession, his collection of record albums worth several hundred dollars. Being somewhat superstitious, he feared that his luck had turned against him and, sure enough, his car was struck by a hit-and-run driver shortly afterwards.

Then in August of the same year, Tom and his father caught a very big fish on a fishing trip and won a prize consisting of a free trip during the season. As he was cleaning the fish to present it to the jury, the line broke and Tom lost the prize fish. But his streak of bad luck was to take on ominous proportions soon after. Two weeks later, Tom Q. died instantly, his friend David died the next day.

Even before the bad news was brought home to Peter Q. and the family, an extraordinary thing happened at their house. The clock in the bedroom stopped suddenly. When Peter checked it and wound it again, he found nothing wrong with it. By then, word of Tom's death had come, and on checking the time, Peter found that the clock had stopped at the very instant of his brother's death.

During the following days, drawers in what used to be their bedroom would open by themselves when there was no one about. This continued for about four weeks, then it stopped again. On the anniversary of Tom's death, Peter, who was then a junior at the university, was doing some studying and using a fountain pen to highlight certain parts in the books. Just then, his mother called him and asked him to help his father with his car. Peter placed the pen inside the book to mark the page and went to help his father. On returning an hour later, he discovered that a picture of his late brother and their family had been placed where Peter had left the pen, and the pen was lying outside the book next to it. No one had been in the house at the time since Peter's wife was out working.

Under the influence of Tom's untimely death and the phenomena taking place at his house, Peter Q. became very interested in life after death and read almost everything he could, talking with many of his friends about the subject, and becoming more and more convinced that man does in some mysterious way survive death. His wife disagreed with him and did not wish to discuss the matter.

One night, while her husband was away from the house, Peter's wife received a telepathic impression concerning continuance of life, and as she did so, a glowing object about the size of a softball appeared next to her in her bed. It was not a dream, for she could see the headlights from passing cars shining on the wall of the room, yet the shining object was still there next to her pillow, stationary and glowing. It eventually disappeared.

Many times since, Peter Q. has felt the presence of his brother, a warm, wonderful feeling; yet it gives him goose bumps all over. As for the real big send-off Tom had wanted from this life, he truly received it. The morning after his accident, a number of friends called the house without realizing that anything had happened to Tom. They had felt a strong urge to call, as if someone had communicated with them telepathically to do so.

Tom Q. was a collector of phonograph records and owned many, even though a large part of his collection had been stolen. The night before his fatal accident, he had played some of these records.

Ghosts of New England

When Peter later checked the record player, he discovered that the last song his brother had played was entitled, "Just One More Day." Of the many Otis Redding recordings his brother owned, why had he chosen that one?

*　　*　　*

Mr. Harold B. is a professional horse trainer who travels a good deal of the time. When he does stay at home, he lives in an old house in a small town in Massachusetts. Prior to moving to New England, he and his wife lived in Ohio, but he was attracted by the Old World atmosphere of New England and decided to settle down in the East. They found a house that was more than two hundred years old, but unfortunately it was in dire need of repair. There was neither electricity nor central heating, and all the rooms were dirty, neglected, and badly in need of renovating. Nevertheless, they liked the general feeling of the house and decided to take it.

The house was in a sad state, mostly because it had been lived in for fifty-five years by a somewhat eccentric couple who had shut themselves off from the world. They would hardly admit anyone to their home, and it was known in town that three of their dogs had died of starvation. Mr. and Mrs. B. moved into the house on Walnut Road in October. Shortly after their arrival, Mrs. B. fractured a leg, which kept her housebound for a considerable amount of time. This was unfortunate since the house needed so much work. Nevertheless, they managed. With professional help, they did the house over from top to bottom, putting in a considerable amount of work and money to make it livable, until it became a truly beautiful house.

Although Mrs. B. is not particularly interested in the occult, she has had a number of psychic experiences in the past, especially of a precognitive nature, and has accepted her psychic powers as a matter of course. Shortly after the couple had moved into the house on Walnut Road, they noticed that there *was* something peculiar about their home.

One night, Mrs. B. was sleeping alone in a downstairs front room off the center entrance hall. Suddenly she was awakened by the sensation of a presence in the room, and as she looked up she saw the figure of a small woman before her bed, looking right at her. She could make out all the details of the woman's face and stature, and noticed that she was wearing a veil, as widows sometimes did in the past. When the apparition became aware of Mrs. B.'s attention, she lifted the veil and spoke to her, assuring her that she was not there to harm her but that she came as a friend. Mrs. B. was too overcome by it all to reply, and before she could gather her wits, the apparition drifted away.

Immediately, Mrs. B. made inquiries in town, and since she was able to give a detailed description of the apparition, it was not long until she knew who the ghost was. The description fit the former owner of the house, Mrs. C., to a tee. Mrs. C. died at age eighty-six, shortly before the B.'s moved into what was her former home. Armed with this information, Mrs. B. braced herself for the presence of an unwanted inhabitant in the house. A short time afterwards, she saw the shadowy outline of what appeared to be a heavy-set person moving along the hall from her bedroom. At first she thought it was her husband so she called out to him, but she soon discovered that her husband was actually upstairs. She then examined her room and discovered that the shades were drawn, so there was no possibility that light from traffic on the road outside could have cast a shadow into the adjoining hall. The shadowy figure she had seen did not, however, look like the outline of the ghost she had earlier encountered in the front bedroom.

While she was wondering about this, she heard the sound of a dog running across the floor. Yet there was no dog to be seen. Evidently her own dog also heard or sensed the ghostly dog's doings because he reacted with visible terror.

Mrs. B. was still wondering about the second apparition when her small grandson came and stayed overnight. He had never been to the house before and had not been told of the stories connected with it. As he was preparing to go to sleep, but still fully conscious, he saw a heavy-set man wearing a red shirt standing before him in his bedroom. This upset him greatly, especially when the man suddenly disappeared without benefit of a door. He described the apparition to his grandparents, who reassured him by telling him a white lie: namely, that he had been dreaming. To this the boy indignantly replied that he had not been dreaming, but, in fact, he had been fully awake. The description given by the boy not only fitted the shadowy outline of the figure Mrs. B. had seen along the corridor, but was a faithful description of the late Mr. C., the former owner of the house.

Although the ghost of Mrs. C. had originally assured the B.'s that she meant no harm and that she had come as a friend, Mrs. B. had her doubts. A number of small items of no particular value disappeared from time to time and were never found again. This was at times when intruders were completely out of the question.

Then Mrs. B. heard the pages of a wallpaper sampler lying on the dining room table being turned one day. Thinking her husband was doing it, she called out to him, only to find that the room was empty. When she located him in another part of the house, he reported having heard the pages being turned also, and this reassured Mrs. B. since she now had her husband's support in the matter of ghosts. It was clear to her that the late owners did not appreciate the many changes they had made in the house. But Mrs. B. also decided that she was not about to be put out of her home by a ghost. The changes had been made for the better, she decided, and the C.'s, even in their present ghostly state, should be grateful for what they had done for the house and not resent them. Perhaps these thoughts somehow reached the two ghosts telepathically; at any rate, the atmosphere in the house became quiet after that.

* * *

Barbara is a young woman with a good background who saw me on a Boston television program and volunteered her own experiences as a result. The following week, she wrote to me.

My family home, in Duxbury, Massachusetts, which is near Plymouth and the home of such notables as Myles Standish and John Alden, is one of the oldest houses in town although we do not know just how old it is.

Last February my brother Edward and his wife Doris and their family moved into the house. Before this my brother Carl and my father were there alone after my mother's death nearly a year ago.

The first occasion of odd happenings was on March 17, St. Patrick's Day. We are a very small part Irish — the name is about all that is left, O'Neil. A friend of mine and I went up to the farm to visit. Shortly after we arrived we heard a noise, which to me sounded like a baby whimpering as it awoke and to my sister-in-law as a woman moaning. I spoke to Doris, something about her baby being awake. She said no and let it pass until later when she told us that she had heard the same noise earlier in the morning and had gone upstairs to check on the baby. As she stood beside the crib, the baby sleeping soundly, she heard the noise again. She then called to the barn to see if all the dogs were accounted for — which they were.

Since this first noticed phenomenon the following things have occurred.

My sister-in-law is keeping a log — I may have omissions.

1. The upstairs door opened and closed (the latch type door) and a shadow filled the whole staircase. It was a calm,

78   *Ghosts of New England*

cloudy day, and the possibility of a draft is somewhat unlikely. Witnessed by Doris.

2. My brother Carl heard a voice saying, "Bring it back." This went on for several minutes but it was clear for the full time.

3. Footsteps upstairs heard by Doris.

4. Doris went into the front room to see the over-stuffed rocker rocking as though someone was in it. After she entered the chair began to stop as though someone got up.

5. July 4, Doris went upstairs and saw the outline of a man which just seemed to disappear.

Before Edward and Doris moved in, Carl and my father were living there alone (all are in the house now). There was no one in the house most of the time since my mother died nearly a year ago. During this time the girl who rents the other house on the farm twice saw the outline of a man over there — once sitting in a chair and another time she woke my brothers about this. She is very jittery about it and as a result does not know about the other things.

I suppose I could go on a bit about the family history. My grandmother traces her ancestry back to Myles Standish and John Alden; my grandfather from Nova Scotia of Scotch-Irish ancestry. I don't know who it was, but someone who lived in the house hanged himself in the barn.

Carl is a sensible, hard-working dairyman who graduated from the University of Massachusetts. Edward is a scoffer since he has observed nothing, recently discharged from the Navy as a lieutenant and is a graduate of Tufts University.

Doris is a very intelligent, levelheaded girl who, before these events, would have called herself a scoffer or disbeliever.

I graduated from Bridgewater Teachers College and at first tried to say that there was a logical explanation to these things but there have just been too many things.

My friend is an intelligent, clear thinking person.

I give you this background on the witnesses, not as a bragger or being vain, but to give you an idea of the type of witnesses. We are not the hysterical, imagining type.

The house has thirteen rooms (not all original) and the ghost seems to roam around at will."

* * *

It has been said that the people of Boston — proper Bostonians — are a breed all their own, polite, erudite, and very determined to have things their own way. I have found that these proper Bostonian ghosts are no different in the afterlife. Some of them may not be exactly erudite, but neither are they insolent or, heaven forbid, dumb.

The Possession of Mrs. F.

Possession for the sake of evil, or for the sake of continuing indefinitely a physical existence, is probably the most feared form of this phenomenon. But there exists a type of possession which is clearly confined in purpose and frequently also in time. In such cases, the possessor takes hold of an individual on the physical plane in order to finish some uncompleted task he or she was unable to accomplish while alive in the physical sense. Once that task has been accomplished, there is no further need for possession, and the possessor withdraws, continuing an existence in the proper dimension, that is, in the nonphysical world.

Nevertheless, there are aspects of this limited and quasi-intelligent possession that are not acceptable to the one to whom it occurs. In the desire to express a need of sorts or finish something that had been started and not ended, the possessor may overlook the desire of the individual not to be possessed, or to be free of such imposed power. Under such circumstances it is advisable to break the hold of the possessor in spite of any good intentions behind the action.

* * *

Virginia F. is an average person of full Irish descent. She describes herself as one of the Black Irish, those who think they are related to the Spanish Armada survivors who took refuge in Ireland in 1588 and later intermingled with the native population. Mrs. F. has five children and lives in a modest home in one of the largest cities in New England. The house was built in February of 1955 and sold to a Mr. and Mrs. J. S. Evidently the home was far from lucky for the first owner whose wife died of cancer in it after about four years. Then it was rented to a Captain M. for about a year. Apparently the good captain wasn't too happy there either for he left. The next owners were C. and E. B. Within a year of acquiring the house they filed for a divorce. A short time later, their oldest son was run over and killed by a truck. At that point, the house passed into the hands of Mrs. F. and her family. A little over two months after they had moved in, her father had a heart attack in the bathroom and died on the way to the hospital. For nine years Mrs. F. and her family managed to live in the house, but their marriage was not a happy one, and it ended in divorce in 1970. Whether or not the tragic atmosphere of the house has any bearing upon what transpired later is hard to tell, but Mrs. F. thought enough of it to advise me of it, and I'm inclined to think that the depressing atmosphere of a house may very well lead to psychic complications. It could very well be that an earlier dwelling stood on the same spot and that some of the older vibrations are clinging to the new house.

On May 25, 1970, Mrs. F.'s divorce was complete. In the fall of the same year she met another man. Francis and his sister Gloria had visited the house after a club meeting, and from that moment on, Mrs. F. and Francis were inseparable. It was love at first sight. For a few weeks, the two went everywhere together, and then the happiness came to a sudden end. Francis was ill with an incurable disease. He knew he did not have long to live. Instead of a wedding, she helped plan his funeral.

The night before he died, he told her he would never leave her and that nothing or no one could ever separate them. He also told her that he would come for her soon. That night he died. And when he died his electric clock stopped exactly at the moment he passed out of the body. For the last day of his life Francis had been attended day and night by Mrs. F. and her two sons, but nothing could have been done to save him.

When the man knew that his time was short, he started to talk with her about death and what he wanted to have done. She had promised him she would buy the lot in the cemetery next to his; faithful to his request, the day after she had buried him, February 14, 1972, she bought the lot next to his.

That day, strange things started to happen in her home. There was, first of all, a picture, which Francis had bought for her, showing the Minuteman on the Lexington Green. The picture would actually fly off the wall, no matter how many times she refastened it. This happened several times and the picture actually flung itself across the room, making a terrific noise. During the three days between Francis' death and his burial, a little valentine she had given him in the hospital would be moved by unseen hands. Someone took it from a ticket, to which it was fastened with a paper clip, and turned it around so that the side on which was written "Love G." was on top. But no one in the house had done it.

After the funeral, Mrs. F. fell asleep, exhausted from the emotional upset. At four o'clock in the morning she woke up to find that a piece of paper she had put in front of her, had been written upon while she was asleep. The words read, "Remember, I love you, Francis."

Realizing that this was a message somehow using her hands to write even though she might not be aware of it, she tried consciously to receive another message by automatic writing a week later. The first line consisted of scribbled letters that made no sense whatsoever.

But the second line became clearer. It was a love message written in the handwriting of the deceased. There was no mistaking it.

When she confided in her family doctor, he shook his head and prescribed sedatives. In her heartbroken state, Mrs. F. remembered how her fiance had promised her a pearl ring for Christmas but had been too sick then to buy it. The matter of the missing pearl ring had been a private joke between them. Two days after the last automatic message, she was putting some things away in the bedroom of her house. She carefully cleaned the top of her dresser and put everything in its proper place. A short time later her oldest daughter asked her to come up to the bedroom. There, on the dresser, was a pearl! How had it gotten there?

"Do these things truly happen, or am I on the verge of a breakdown?" Mrs. F. asked herself. She remembered how she had written to me some years ago concerning some ESP experiences she had had. Again she got in touch with me, this time for help. "Help me, please, to understand. And if you tell me that I'm losing my mind," she wrote, "then I'll go to the hospital." But I assured her that she was not insane. All she really wanted was to be with her Francis at this point.

Mrs. F. was indeed in a fix. There was nothing wrong with her love relationship, but Francis's promise to take her over to his side of life was another matter. I was convinced that those who were guiding him now would also instruct him accordingly. Gently I explained to Mrs. F. that love cannot fully bridge the gap between the two worlds of existence.

There is a time for them to be joined, but for the present she belonged to the world of the body and must continue to live in it as best she could. When she accepted her true position and also her renewed responsibility towards her children, the hold — which the deceased had had upon her for a while after his passing — lessened. It was as if Francis had understood that his business had indeed been finished. The knowledge of his continued existence in another dimension was all he wanted to convey to his one and only love. That done, he could await her coming in due time in the conviction that they would be together without the shadow of possession between them.

The Ghost at
Cap'n Grey's

Some of the best leads regarding a good ghost story come to me as the result of my having appeared on one of many television or radio programs, usually discussing a book dealing with the subject matter for which I am best known — psychic phenomena of one kind or another. So it happened that one of my many appearances on the Bob Kennedy television show in Boston drew unusually heavy mail from places as far away as other New England states and even New York.

Now if there is one thing ghosts don't really care much about it is time — to them everything is suspended in a timeless dimension where the intensity of their suffering or problem remains forever constant and alive. After all, they are unable to let go of what it is that ties them to a specific location, otherwise they would not be what we so commonly (and perhaps a little callously) call ghosts. I am mentioning this as a way of explaining why, sometimes, I cannot respond as quickly as I would like to when someone among the living reports a case of a haunting that needs to be looked into. Reasons were and are now mainly lack of time but more likely lack of funds to organize a team and go after the case. Still, by and large, I do manage to show up in time and usually manage to resolve the situation.

Thus it happened that I received a letter dated August 4, 1966, sent to me via station WBZ-TV in Boston, from the owner of Cap'n Grey's Smorgasbord, an inn located in Barnstable on Cape Cod. The owner, Mr. Lennart Svensson, had seen me on the show and asked me to get in touch.

"We have experienced many unusual happenings here. The building in which our restaurant and guest house is located was built in 1716 and was formerly a sea captain's residence," Svensson wrote.

I'm a sucker for sea captains haunting their old houses so I wrote back asking for details. Mr. Svensson replied a few weeks later, pleased to have aroused my interest. Both he and his wife had seen the apparition of a young woman, and their eldest son had also felt an unseen presence; guests in their rooms also mentioned unusual happenings. It appeared that when the house was first built the foundation had been meant as a fortification against Indian attacks. Rumor has it, Mr. Svensson informed me, that the late sea captain had been a slave trader and sold slaves on the premises.

Svensson and his wife, both of Swedish origin, had lived on the Cape in the early thirties, later moved back to Sweden, to return in 1947. After a stint working in various restaurants in New York, they acquired the inn on Cape Cod.

I decided a trip to the Cape was in order. I asked Sybil Leek to accompany me as the medium. Mr. Svensson explained that the inn would close in October for the winter, but he, and perhaps other witnesses to the phenomena, could be seen even after that date, should I wish to come up then. But it was not until June 1967, the following year, that I finally managed to get our act together, so to speak, and I contacted Mr. Svensson to set a date for our visit. Unfortunately, he had since sold the inn and, as he put it, the new owner was not as interested in the ghost as he was, so there was no way for him to arrange for our visit now.

But Mr. Svensson did not realize how stubborn a man I can be when I want to do something. I never gave up on this case, and decided to wait a little and then approach the new owners. Before I could do so, however, the new owner saw fit to get in touch with me instead. He referred to the correspondence between Mr. Svensson and myself, and explained that at the time I had wanted to come up, he had been in the process of redoing the inn for its opening. That having taken place several weeks ago, it would appear that "we have experienced evidence of the spirit on several occasions, and I now feel we should look into this matter as soon as possible." He invited us to come on up whenever it was convenient, preferably yesterday.

The new owner turned out to be an attorney named Jack Furman of Hyannis, and a very personable man at that. When I wrote we would indeed be pleased to meet him, and the ghost or ghosts, as the case might be, he sent us all sorts of information regarding flights and offered to pick us up at the airport. Mr. Furman was not shy in reporting his own experiences since he had taken over the house.

There has been on one occasion an umbrella mysteriously stuck into the stairwell in an open position. This was observed by my employee, Thaddeus B. Ozimek. On another occasion when the Inn was closed in the evening early, my manager returned to find the front door bolted from *the inside* which appeared strange since no one was in the building. At another time, my chef observed that the heating plant went off at 2:30, and the serviceman, whom I called the next day, found that a fuse was removed from the fuse box. At 2:30 in the morning, obviously, no one that we know of was up and around to do this. In addition, noises during the night have been heard by occupants of the Inn.

I suggested in my reply that our little team consisting, as it would, of medium (and writer) Sybil Leek, Catherine (my wife at the time), and myself, should spend the night at the Inn as good ghost hunters do. I also requested that the former owner, Mr. Svensson, be present for further questioning, as well as any direct witnesses to phenomena. On the other hand, I delicately suggested that no one not concerned with the case should be present, keeping in mind some occasions where my investigations had been turned into entertainment by my hosts to amuse and astound neighbors and friends.

In the end it turned out to be best to come by car as we had other projects to look into en route, such as Follins Pond, where we eventually discovered the possibility of a submerged Viking ship at the bottom of the pond. The date for our visit was to be August 17, 1967 — a year and two weeks after the case first came to my attention. But not much of a time lag, the way it is with ghosts.

When we arrived at the Inn, after a long and dusty journey, the sight that greeted us was well worth the trip. There, set back from a quiet country road amid tall, aged trees, sat an impeccable white colonial house, two stories high with an attic, nicely surrounded by a picket fence, and an old bronze and iron lamp at the corner. The windows all had their wooden shutters opened to the outside and the place presented such a picture of peace it was difficult to realize we had come here to confront a disturbance. The house was empty, as we soon realized, because the new owner had not yet allowed guests to return — considering what the problems were!

Quickly, we unburdened ourselves of our luggage, each taking a room upstairs, then returned to the front of the house to begin our usual inspection. Sybil Leek now let go of her conscious self the more to immerse herself in the atmosphere and potential presences of the place.

"There is something in the bedroom . . . in the attic," Sybil said immediately as we climbed the winding stairs. "I thought just now someone was pushing my hair up from the back," she then added.

Mr. Furman had, of course, come along for the investigation. At this point we all saw a flash of light in the middle of the room. None of us was frightened by it, not even the lawyer who by now had taken the presence of the supernatural in his house in his stride.

We then proceeded downstairs again, with Sybil assuring us that whatever it was that perturbed her up in the attic did not seem to be present downstairs. With that we came to a locked door, a door that Mr. Furman assured us that had not been opened in a long time. When we managed to get it open, it led us to the downstairs office or the room now used as such. Catherine, ever the alert artist and designer that she was, noticed that a door had been barred from the inside, almost as if someone had once been kept in that little room. Where did this particular door lead to, I asked Mr. Furman. It appeared it led to a narrow corridor and finally came out into the fireplace in the large main room.

"Someone told me if I ever dug up the fireplace," Mr. Furman intoned significantly, "I might find something."

What that something would be, was left to our imagination. Mr. Furman added that his informant had hinted at some sort of valuables, but Sybil immediately added, "bodies . . . you may find bodies."

She described, psychically, many people suffering in the house, and a secret way out of the house — possibly from the captain's slave trading days?

Like a doctor examining a patient, I then examined the walls both in the little room and the main room and found many hollow spots. A bookcase turned out to be a false front. Hidden passages seemed to suggest themselves. Quite obviously, Mr. Furman was not about to tear open the walls to find them. But Sybil was right: the house was honeycombed with areas not visible to the casual observer.

Sybil insisted we seat ourselves around the fireplace, and I insisted that the ghost, if any, should contact us there rather than our trying to chase the elusive phantom from room to room. "A way out of the house is very important," Sybil said, and I couldn't help visualizing the unfortunate slaves the good (or not so good) captain had held captive in this place way back.

But when nothing much happened, we went back to the office, where I discovered that the front portion of the wall seemed to block off another room beyond it, not accounted for when measuring the outside walls. When we managed to pry it open, we found a stairwell, narrow though it was, where apparently a flight of stairs had once been. I asked for a flashlight. Catherine shone it up the shaft: we found ourselves below a toilet in an upstairs bathroom! No ghost here.

We sat down again, and I invited the presence, whomever it was, to manifest. Immediately Sybil remarked she felt a young boy around the place, a hundred and fifty years ago. As she went more and more into a trance state, Sybil mentioned the name Chet . . . someone who wanted to be safe from an enemy . . . Carson . . .

"Let him speak," I said.

"Carson . . . 1858 . . . " Sybil replied, now almost totally entranced as I listened carefully for words coming from her in halting fashion.

"I will fight . . . Charles . . . the child is missing . . . "

"Whom will you fight? Who took the child?" I asked in return.

"Chicopee . . . child is dead."

"Whose house is this?"

"Fort . . . "

"Whose is it?"

"Carson . . . "

"Are you Carson?"

"Captain Carson."

"What regiment?"

"Belvedere . . . cavalry . . . 9th . . . "

"Where is the regiment stationed?"

There was no reply.

"Who commanded the regiment?" I insisted.

"Wainwright . . . Edward Wainwright . . . commander."

"How long have you been here?"

"Four years."

"Where were you born?"

"Montgomery . . . Massachusetts."

"How old are you now?"

There was no reply.

"Are you married?"

"My son . . . Tom . . . ten . . . "

"What year was he born in?"

"Forty . . . seven . . . "

"Your wife's name?"

"Gina . . . "

"What church do you go to?"

"I don't go."

"What church do you belong to?"

"She is . . . of Scottish background . . . Scottish kirk."

"Where is the kirk located?"

"Six miles . . . "

"What is the name of this village we are in now?"

"Chicopee . . . "

Further questioning gave us this information: that "the enemy" had taken his boy, and the enemy were the Iroquois. This was his fort and he was to defend it. I then began, as I usually do, when exorcism is called for, to speak of the passage of time and the need to realize that the entity communicating through the medium was aware of the true situation in this respect. Did Captain Carson realize that time had passed since the boy had disappeared?

"Oh yes," he replied. "Four years."

"No, a hundred and seven years," I replied.

Once again I established that he was Captain Carson, and there was a river nearby and Iroquois were the enemy. Was he aware that there were "others" here besides himself.

He did not understand this. Would he want me to help him find his son since they had both passed over and should be able to find each other there?

"I need permission . . . from Wainwright . . . "

As I often do in such cases, I pretended to speak for Wainwright and granted him the permission. A ghost, after all, is not a rational human being but an entity existing in a delusion where only emotions count.

"Are you now ready to look for your son?"

"I am ready."

"Then I will send a messenger to help you find him," I said, "but you must call out to your son . . . in a loud voice."

The need to reach out to a loved one is of cardinal importance in the release of a trapped spirit, commonly called a ghost.

"John Carson is dead . . . but not dead forever," he said in a faint voice.

"You lived here in 1858, but this is 1967," I reminded him.

"You are mad!"

"No, I'm not mad. Touch your forehead . . . you will see this is not the body you are accustomed to. We have lent you a body to communicate with us. But it is not yours."

Evidently touching a woman's head did jolt the entity from his beliefs. I decided to press on.

"Go from this house and join your loved ones who await you outside . . ."

A moment later Captain Carson had slipped away and a sleepy Sybil Leek opened her eyes.

I now turned to Mr. Furman, who had watched the proceedings with mounting fascination. Could he corroborate any of the information that had come to us through the entranced medium?

"This house was built on the foundations of an Indian fort," he confirmed, "to defend the settlers against the Indians."

"Were there any Indians here in 1858?"

"There are Indians here even now," Furman replied. "We have an Indian reservation at Mashpee, near here, and on Martha's Vineyard there is a tribal chief and quite a large Indian population."

He also confirmed having once seen a sign in the western part of Massachusetts that read "Montgomery" — the place Captain Carson had claimed as his birthplace. Also that a Wainwright family was known to have lived in an area not far from where we were now. However, Mr. Furman had no idea of any military personnel by that name.

"Sybil mentioned a river in connection with this house." Furman said, "And, yes, there is a river running through the house, it is still here."

Earlier Sybil had drawn a rough map of the house as it was in the past, from her psychic viewpoint, a house surrounded by a high fence. Mr. Furman pronounced the drawing amazingly accurate — especially as Sybil had not set foot on the property or known about it until our actual arrival.

"My former secretary, Carole E. Howes, and her family occupied this house," Mr. Furman explained when I turned my attention to the manifestations themselves. "They operated this house as an Inn twenty years ago, and often had unusual things happen here as she grew up, but it did not seem to bother them. Then the house passed into the hands of a Mrs. Nielson; then Mr. Svensson took over. But he did not speak of the phenomena until about a year and a half ago. The winter of 1965 he was shingling the roof, and he was just coming in from the roof on the second floor balcony on a cold day — he had left the window ajar and secured — when suddenly he heard the window sash come down. He turned around on the second floor platform and he saw the young girl, her hair windswept behind her. She was wearing white. He could not see anything below the waist, and he confronted her for a short period, but could not bring himself to talk — and she went away. His wife was in the kitchen sometime later, in the afternoon, when she felt the presence of someone in the room. She turned around and saw an older man dressed in black at the other end of the kitchen. She ran out of the kitchen and never went back in again.

"The accountant John Dillon's son was working in the kitchen one evening around ten. Now some of these heavy pots were hanging there on pegs from the ceiling. Young Dillon told his father two of them lifted themselves up from the ceiling, unhooked themselves from the pegs, and came down on the floor."

Did any guests staying at the Inn during Svensson's ownership complain of any unusual happenings?

"There was this young couple staying at what Mr. Svensson called the honeymoon suite," Mr. Furman replied. "At 6:30 in the morning, the couple heard three knocks at the door, three loud, distinct knocks, and when they opened the door, there was no one there. This sort of thing had happened before."

Another case involved a lone diner who complained to Svensson that "someone" was pushing him from his chair at the table in the dining room onto another chair, but since he did not see another person, how could this be? Svensson hastily had explained that the floor was a bit rickety and that was probably the cause.

The Ghost at Cap'n Grey's   95

Furman then recounted the matter of the lock: he and a young man who worked with him had left the Inn to bring the chef, who had become somewhat difficult that day, home to his own place. When Mr. Furman's assistant returned to the Inn at 2:30 in the morning, the door would not open, and the key would not work. After he had climbed into the house through an upstairs window, he found to his amazement that the door had been locked *from the inside*.

The story gave me a chill: that very day, after our arrival, nearly the same thing happened to us — except that we did not have to climb to the upper floor to get in but managed to enter through a rear door! Surely, someone did not exactly want us in the house.

The chef, by the way, had an experience of his own. The heating system is normally quite noisy, but one night it suddenly stopped and the heat went off. When the repair crew came the next day they discovered that a fuse had been physically removed from the fuse box, which in turn stopped the heating system from operating. The house was securely locked at that time so no one from the outside could have done this.

The famous case of an umbrella being stuck into the ceiling of the upstairs hall was confirmed by the brother of the young man, Mr. Bookstein, living in the house. He also pointed out to us that the Chicopee Indians were indeed in this area, so Sybil's trance utterances made a lot of sense.

"There was an Indian uprising in Massachusetts as late as the middle of the nineteenth century," he confirmed, giving more credence to the date, 1858, that had come through Sybil.

Was the restless spirit of the captain satisfied with our coming? Did he and his son meet up in the Great Beyond? Whatever came of our visit, nothing further has been heard of any disturbances at Cap'n Grey's Inn in Barnstable.

The Strange Case of Mrs. C.'s Late but Lively Husband

Death is not the end, no, definitely not. At least not for Mr. C. who lived the good life in a fair sized city in Rhode Island. But then he died, or so it would appear on the record. But Mrs. C. came to consult me about the very unusual complaint of her late husband's continuing attentions.

When someone dies unexpectedly, or in the prime of his physical life, and finds that he can no longer express his sexual appetite physically in the world into which he has been suddenly catapulted, he may indeed look around for someone through whom he can express this appetite on the earth plane. It is then merely a matter of searching out opportunities, regardless of personalities involved. It is quite conceivable that a large percentage of the unexplained or inexplicable sexual attacks by otherwise meek, timid, sexually defensive individuals upon members of the opposite sex — or even the same sex — may be due to sudden possession by an entity of this kind. This is even harder to prove objectively than are some of the murder cases involving individuals who do not recall what they have done and are for all practical purposes normal human beings before and after the crime. But I am convinced that the influence of discarnates can indeed be exercised upon susceptible individuals — that is to say, appropriately mediumistic individuals. It also appears from my studies that the most likely recipients of this doubtful honor are those who are sexually weak or inactive. Evidently the unused sexual energies are particularly useful to the discarnate entities for their own gains. There really doesn't seem to be any way in which one can foretell such attacks or prevent them, except, perhaps, by leading a sexually healthy and balanced life. *Those who are fulfilled in their natural drives on the earth plane are least likely to suffer from such invasions.*

On the other hand, there exist cases of sexual possession involving two partners who knew each other before on the earth plane. One partner was cut short by death, either violently or prematurely, and would now seek to continue a pleasurable relationship of the flesh from the new dimension. Deprived of a physical body to express such desires, however, the deceased partner would then find it rather difficult to express the physical desires to the partner remaining on the earth plane. With sex it certainly takes two, and if the remaining partner is not willing, then difficulties will have to be reckoned with. An interesting case came to my attention a few months ago. Mrs. Anna C. lives with her several children in a comparatively new house in the northeastern United States. She bought the house eighteen months after her husband had passed away. Thus there was no connection between the late husband and the new house. Nevertheless, her husband's passing was by no means the end of their relationship.

"My husband died five years ago this past September. Ever since then he has not let me have a peaceful day," she explained in desperation, seeking my help.

Two months after her husband had died, she saw him coming to her in a dream complaining that she had buried him alive. He explained that he wasn't really dead, and that it was all her fault and her family's fault that he died in the first place.

Mr. C. had lived a rather controversial life, drinking regularly and frequently staying away from home. Thus the relationship between himself and his wife was far from ideal. Nevertheless, there was a strong bond between them.

"In other dreams he would tell me that *he was going to have sex relations with me whether I wanted him to or not.* He would try to grab me and I would run all through the house with him chasing after me. I never let him get hold of me. He was like that when he was alive, too. The most important thing in life to him was sex, and he didn't care how or where he got it. Nothing else mattered to him," she complained, describing vividly how the supposedly dead husband had apparently still a great deal of life in him.

"He then started climbing on the bed and walking up and down on it and scaring me half to death. I didn't know what it was or what to do about it," she said, shaking like a leaf.

When Mr. C. could not get his wife to cooperate willingly, he apparently got mad. To express his displeasure, he caused all sorts of havoc around the household. He would tear a pair of stockings every day for a week, knock things over, and even go to the place where his mother-in-law worked as a cook, causing seemingly inexplicable phenomena to occur there as well. He appeared to an aunt in Indiana and told her to mind her own business and stay out of his personal relationship with Mrs. C. (It was the aunt who tried to get rid of him and his influences by performing a spiritualist ritual at the house.) Meanwhile, Mr. C. amused himself by setting alarm clocks to go off at the wrong times or stopping them altogether, moving objects from their accustomed places or making them disappear altogether, only to return them several days later to everyone's surprise. In general, he behaved like a good *poltergeist* should. But it didn't endear him any more to his erstwhile wife.

When Mrs. C. rejected his attentions, he started to try to possess his ten-year-old daughter. He came to her in dreams and told her that her mother wasn't really knowledgeable about anything. He tried everything in his power to drive a wedge between the little girl and her mother. As a result of this, the little girl turned more and more away from her mother, and no matter how Mrs. C. tried to explain things to her, she found the little girl's mind made up under the influence of her late father.

In a fit of destructiveness, the late Mr. C. then started to work on the other children, creating such a state of havoc in the household that Mrs. C. did not know where to turn any longer. Then the psychic aunt from Indiana came to New England to try to help matters. Sure enough, Mr. C. appeared to her and the two had a cozy talk. He explained that he was very unhappy where he was and was having trouble getting along with the people over there. To this, the aunt replied she would be very happy to help him get to a higher plane if that was what he wanted. But that wasn't it, he replied. He just wanted to stay where he was. The aunt left for home. Now the children, one by one, became unmanageable, and Mrs. C. assumed that her late husband was interfering with their proper education and discipline. "I am fighting an unseen force and cannot get through to the children," she explained.

Her late husband did everything to embarrass her. She was working as a clerk at St. Francis' rectory in her town, doing some typing. It happened to be December 24, 1971, Christmas Eve. All of a sudden she heard a thud in her immediate vicinity and looked down to the floor. A heavy dictionary was lying at her feet. The book had been on the shelf only a fraction of a second before. A co-worker wondered what was up. She was hard pressed to explain the presence of the dictionary on the floor since it had been on the shelf in back of them only a moment before. But she knew very well how the dictionary came to land at her feet.

Mr. C. prepared special Christmas surprises for his wife. She went to her parents' house to spend the holiday. During that time her nephew George was late for work since his alarm had not worked properly. On inspection it turned out that someone had stuck a pencil right through the clock. As soon as the pencil was removed, the clock started to work again. On investigation it turned out that no one had been near the clock, and when the family tried to place the pencil into the clock, as they had found it, no one could do it. The excitement made Mrs. C. so ill she went to bed. That was no way to escape Mr. C.'s attentions, however. The day before New Year's Eve, her late husband got to her, walking up and down on the bed itself. Finally she told him to leave her and the children alone, to go where he belonged. She didn't get an answer. But phenomena continued in the house, so she asked her aunt to come back once again. This time the aunt from Indiana brought oil with her and put it on each of the children and Mrs. C. herself. Apparently it worked, or so it seemed to Mrs. C. But her late husband was merely changing his tactics. A few days later she was sure that he was trying to get into one of the children to express himself further since he could no longer get at her. She felt she would be close to a nervous breakdown if someone would not help her get rid of the phenomenon and, above all, break her husband's hold on her. "I am anxious to have him sent on up where he can't bother anyone any more," she explained.

Since I could not go immediately, and the voice on the telephone sounded as if its owner could not hold out a single day more, I asked Ethel Johnson Meyers, my mediumistic friend, to go out and see what she could do. Mrs. C. had to go to Mrs. Meyers' house for a personal sitting first. A week later Ethel came down to Mrs. C.'s house to continue her work. What Mrs. Meyers discovered was somewhat of a surprise to Mrs. C. and to myself. It was Ethel's contention that the late husband, while still in the flesh, had himself been the victim of possession and had done the many unpleasant things (of which he was justly accused) during his lifetime, not of his own volition but under the direction of another entity. That the possessor was himself possessed seemed like a novel idea to me, one neither Mrs. Meyers nor I could prove. Far more important was the fact that Mrs. Meyers' prayers and commands to the unseen entity seemed to have worked, for he walks up and down Mrs. C.'s bed no more, and all is quiet. I believe the hold Mr. C. had upon his wife after his death was so strong because of an unconscious desire on her part to continue their relationship. Even though she abhorred him — and the idea of being sexually possessed by a man who had lost his physical body in the usual way — something within her, perhaps deeply buried within her, may have wanted the continuous sexual attention he had bestowed upon her while still in the body.

A Plymouth Ghost

Iam not talking about *the* Plymouth where the Pilgrims landed but another Plymouth. This one is located in New Hampshire, in a part of the state that is rather lonely and sparsely settled even today. If you really want to get away from it all — whatever it may be — this is a pretty good bet. I am mentioning this because a person living in this rural area isn't likely to have much choice in the way of entertainment, unless of course you provide it yourself. But I am getting ahead of my story.

I was first contacted about this case in August 1966 when a young lady named Judith Elliott, who lived in Bridgeport, Connecticut, at the time, informed me of the goings-on in her cousin's country house located in New Hampshire. Judith asked if I would be interested in contacting Mrs. Chester Fuller regarding these matters? What intrigued me about the report was not the usual array of footfalls, presences, and the house cat staring at someone unseen — but the fact that Mrs. Fuller apparently had seen a ghost and identified him from a book commemorating the Plymouth town bicentennial.

When I wrote back rather enthusiastically, Miss Elliott forwarded my letter to her cousin, requesting more detailed and chronological information. But it was not until well into the following year that I finally got around to making plans for a visit. Ethel Johnson Meyers, the late medium, and my ex-wife Catherine, always interested in spooky houses since she used to illustrate some of my books, accompanied me. Mrs. Fuller, true to my request, supplied me with all that she knew of the phenomena themselves, who experienced them, and such information about former owners of the house and the house itself as she could garner. Here, in her own words, is that report, which of course I kept from the medium at all times so as not to influence her or give her prior knowledge of house and circumstances. Mrs. Fuller's report is as follows:

Location: The house is located at 38 Merrill Street in the town of Plymouth, New Hampshire. To reach the house, you leave Throughway 93 at the first exit for Plymouth. When you reach the set of lights on Main Street, turn right and proceed until you reach the blue Sunoco service station, then take a sharp left onto Merrill Street. The house is the only one with white picket snow fence out front. It has white siding with a red front door and a red window box and is on the right hand side of the street.

1. The first time was around the middle of June — about a month after moving in. It was the time of day when lights are needed inside, but it is still light outside. This instance was in the kitchen and bathroom. The bathroom and dining room are in an addition onto the kitchen. The doors to both rooms go out of the kitchen beside of each other, with just a small wall space between. At that time we had our kitchen table in that space. I was getting supper, trying to put the food on the table and keep two small

children (ages 2 and 5) off the table. As I put the potatoes on the table, I swung around from the sink toward the bathroom door. I thought I saw someone in the bathroom. I looked and saw a man. He was standing about half-way down the length of the room. He was wearing a brown plaid shirt, dark trousers with suspenders, and he [wore] glasses with the round metal frames. He was of medium height, a little on the short side, not fat and not thin but a good build, a roundish face, and he was smiling. Suddenly he was gone, no disappearing act or anything fancy, just gone, as he had come.

2. Footsteps. There are footsteps in other parts of the house. If I am upstairs, the footsteps are downstairs. If I am in the kitchen, they are in the livingroom, etc. These were scattered all through the year, in all seasons, and in the daytime. It was usually around 2 or 3 and always on a sunny day, as I recall.

3. Winter — late at night. Twice we (Seth and I) heard a door shutting upstairs. (Seth is an elderly man who stays with us now. When we first moved here he was not staying with us. His wife was a distant cousin to my father. I got acquainted with them when I was in high school. I spent a lot of time at their house and his wife and I became quite close. She died 11 years ago and since then Seth has stayed at his son's house, a rooming house, and now up here. He spent a lot of time visiting us before he moved in.) Only one door in the bedrooms upstairs works right, and that is the door to my bedroom. I checked the kids that night to see if they were up or awake, but they had not moved. My husband was also sound asleep. The door was already shut, as my husband had shut it tight when he went to bed to keep out the sound of the television. The sound of the door was very

distinct — the sound of when it first made contact, then the latch clicking in place, and then the thud as it came in contact with the casing. Everything was checked out — anything that was or could be loose and have blown and banged, or anything that could have fallen down. Nothing had moved. The door only shut once during that night, but did it again later on in the winter.

4. The next appearance was in the fall. I was pregnant at the time. I lost the baby on the first of November, and this happened around the first of October. Becky Sue, my youngest daughter, was 3 at the time. She was asleep in her crib as it was around midnight or later. I was asleep in my bedroom across the hall. I woke up and heard her saying, "Mommy, what are you doing in my bedroom?" She kept saying that until I thought I had better answer her or she would begin to be frightened. I started to say "I'm not in your room," and as I did I started to turn over and I saw what seemed to be a woman in a long white nightgown in front of my bedroom door. In a flash it was gone out into the hall. All this time Becky had been saying, "Mommy, what are you doing in my room?" As the image disappeared out in the hall, Becky changed her question to, "Mommy, what were you doing in my bedroom?" Then I thought that if I told her I wasn't in her room that she would really be scared. All this time I thought that it was Kimberly, my older daughter, getting up, and I kept waiting for her to speak to me. Becky was still sounding like a broken record with her questions. Finally I heard "It" take two steps down, turn a corner, and take three steps more. Then I went into Becky's room and told her that I had forgotten what I had gone into her room for and to lie down and go to sleep, which she did. All this time Kim had not moved. The next morning I was

telling Seth (who was living with us now) about it, and I remembered about the footsteps going downstairs. I wondered if Becky had heard them too, so I called her out into the kitchen and asked her where I went after I left her room. She looked at me as if I had lost my mind and said, "Downstairs!"

5. This was in the winter, around 2. Seth was helping me make the beds upstairs as they had been skipped for some reason. We heard footsteps coming in from the playroom across the kitchen and a short way into the hall. We both thought it was Becky Sue who was playing outdoors. She comes in quite frequently for little odds and ends. Still no one spoke. We waited for a while expecting her to call to me. Finally, when she did not call, I went downstairs to see what she wanted, and there was no one there. I thought that maybe she had gone back out, but there was no snow on the floor or tracks of any kind. This was also on a very sunny day.

6. This was also late at night in 1965, around 11. I was putting my husband's lunch up when there was a step right behind me. That scared me, although I do not know why; up until that time I had never had any fear. Maybe it was because it was right behind my back and the others had always been at a distance or at least in front of me.

I cannot remember anything happening since then. Lately there have been noises as if someone was in the kitchen or dining room while I was in the livingroom, but I cannot be sure of that. It sounds as if something was swishing, but I cannot *definitely* say that it is not the sounds of an old house.

History of House and Background of Previous Owners

The history of the house and its previous owners is

very hard to get. We bought the house from Mrs. Ora Jacques. Her husband had bought it from their son who had moved to Florida. The husband was going to do quite a bit of remodeling and then sell it. When he died, Mrs. Jacques rented it for a year and then sold it.

Mr. Jacques' son bought it from a man who used to have a doughnut shop and did his cooking in a back room, so I have been told. There was a fire in the back that was supposedly started from the fat. They bought the house from Mrs. Emma Thompson, who, with her husband, had received the house for caring for a Mr. Woodbury Langdon, and by also giving him a small sum of money. Mrs. Thompson always gave people the impression that she was really a countess and that she had a sister in Pennsylvania who would not have anything to do with her because of her odd ways.

Mrs. Thompson moved to Rumney where she contracted pneumonia about six months later and died.

Mr. and Mrs. Thompson moved in to take care of Mr. Woodbury Langdon after he kicked out Mr. and Mrs. Dinsmore. (Mr. Cushing gave me the following information. He lives next door, and has lived there since 1914 or 1918).

He was awakened by a bright flash very early in the morning. Soon he could see that the top room (tower room) was all afire. He got dressed, called the firemen, and ran over to help. He looked in the window of what is now our dining room but was then Mr. Langdon's bedroom. (Mr. Langdon was not able to go up and down stairs because of his age.) He pounded on the window trying to wake Mr. Langdon up. Through the window he could see Mr. and Mrs. Dinsmore standing in the doorway between the kitchen and the bedroom. They were laughing and Mr. Dinsmore had an oil can in his hand. All this time Mr. Langdon was sound asleep. Mr. Cushing got angry and began pounding harder and harder. Just as he began to open the window Mr. Langdon woke up and Mr. Cushing helped him out the window. He said that no one would believe his story, even the insurance company. Evidently Mr. Langdon did because soon after he kicked the Dinsmores out and that was when Mr. and Mrs. Thompson came to take care of him. Around 1927 he came down with pneumonia. He had that for two days and then he went outdoors without putting on any jacket or sweater. Mrs. Thompson ran out and brought him back in. She put him back in bed and warmed him up with coffee and wrapped him in wool blankets. He seemed better until around midnight. Then he began moaning. He kept it up until around 3, when he died.

Mr. Langdon was married twice. His first wife and his eighteen-year-old son died [of] typhoid fever. He had the wells examined and found that it came from them. He convinced his father to invest his money in putting in the first water works for the town of Plymouth. At that time he lived across town on Russell Street.

He later married a woman by the name of Donna. He worshipped her and did everything he could to please her. He remodeled the house. That was when he added on the bathroom and bedroom (dining room). He also built the tower room so that his wife could look out over the town. He also had a big estate over to Squam Lake that he poured out money on. All this time she was running around with anyone she could find. Mr. Cushing believes that he knew it deep down but refused to let himself believe it. She died,

Mr. Cushing said, from the things she got from the thing she did! He insists that it was called leprosy. In the medical encyclopedia it reads, under leprosy, "differential diag: tuberculosis and esp. syphilis are the two disease most likely to be considered." She died either in this house or at the estate on the lake. She was buried in the family plot in Trinity Cemetery in Holderness. She has a small headstone with just one name on it, Donna. There is a large spire shaped monument in the center of the lot, with the family's names on it and their relationship. The name of Woodbury Langdon's second wife is completely eliminated from the stone. There is nothing there to tell who she was or why she is buried there. This has puzzled me up to now, because, as she died around 1911, and he did not die until around 1927, he had plenty of time to have her name and relationship added to the family stone. Mr. Cushing thinks that, after her death, Mr. Langdon began to realize more and more what she was really like. He has the impression that Mr. Langdon was quite broke at the time of his death.

I cannot trace any more of the previous owners, as I cannot trace the house back any farther than around 1860. Mr. Langdon evidently bought and sold houses like other men bought and sold horses. If this is the house I believe it to be, it was on the road to Rumney and had to be moved in a backward position to where it is now. They had something like six months later to move the barn back. Then they had to put in a street going from the house up to the main road. They also had to put a fence up around the house. This property *did* have a barn, and there was a fence here. There is a small piece of it left. The deeds from there just go around in circles.

The man who I think the ghost is, is Mr. Woodbury

Langdon. I have asked people around here what Mr. Langdon looked like and they describe him VERY MUCH as the man I saw in the bathroom. The man in the bicentennial book was his father. There is something in his face that was in the face of the "ghost."

I have two children. They are: Kimberly Starr, age 9 years and Rebecca Sue, age 6 years. Kim's birthday is on April 2 and Becky's is on August 10.

I was born and brought up on a farm 4½ miles out in the country in the town of Plymouth. My father believes in spirits, sort of, but not really. My mother absolutely does not.

I carried the business course and the college preparatory course through my four years of high school. I had one year of nurses' training. I was married when I was 20, in June, and Kim was born the next April.

P.S. We have a black cat who has acted queer at times in the past.
1. He would go bounding up the stairs only to come to an abrupt halt at the head of the stairs. He would sit there staring at presumably empty space, and then take off as if he had never stopped.
2. Sometimes he stood at the bathroom door and absolutely refused to go in.
3. He had spells of sitting in the hallway and staring up the stairs, not moving a muscle. Then suddenly he would relax and go on his way.

*　*　*

We finally settled on August 12, a Saturday, in 1967, to have a go at Mr. Langdon or whoever it was that haunted the house, because Miss Elliott was getting married in July and Mrs. Fuller wanted very much to be present.

Eleanor Fuller greeted us as we arrived, and led us into the house. As usual Ethel began to sniff around, and I just followed her, tape recorder running and camera at the ready. We followed her up the stairs to the upper floor, where Ethel stopped at the bedroom on the right, which happened to be decorated in pink.

"I get an older woman wearing glasses," Ethel said cautiously as she was beginning to pick up psychic leads, "and a man wearing a funny hat."

I pressed Ethel to be more specific about the "funny hat" and what period hat. The man seemed to her to belong to the early 1800s. She assured me it was not this century. She then complained about a cold spot, and when I stepped into it I too felt it. Since neither doors nor windows could be held responsible for the strong cold draft we felt, we knew that its origin was of a psychic nature, as it often is when there are entities present.

I asked Ethel to describe the woman she felt present. "She is lying down . . . and I get a pain in the chest," she said, picking up the spirit's condition. "The eyes are closed!"

We left the room and went farther on. Ethel grabbed her left shoulder as if in pain.

"She is here with me, looking at me," Ethel said.

"She's been here."

"Why is she still here?" I asked.

"I get a sudden chill when you asked that," Ethel replied.

"She tells me to go left . . . I am having difficulty walking . . . I think this woman had that difficulty."

We were walking down the stairs, when Ethel suddenly became a crone and had difficulty managing them. The real Ethel was as spry and fast as the chipmunks that used to roam around her house in Connecticut.

"I think she fell down these stairs," Ethel said and began to cough. Obviously, she was being impressed by a very sick person.

We had barely got Ethel to a chair when she slipped into full trance and the transition took place. Her face became distorted as in suffering, and a feeble voice tried to manifest through her, prodded by me to be clearer.

"Lander . . . or something . . ." she mumbled.

What followed was an absolutely frightening realization by an alien entity inside Ethel's body that the illness she was familiar with no longer existed now. At the same time, the excitement of this discovery made it difficult for the spirit to speak clearly, and we were confronted with a series of grunts and sighs.

Finally, I managed to calm the entity down by insisting she needed to relax in order to be heard.

"Calm . . . calm . . ." she said and cried, "good . . . he knows . . . he did that . . . for fifty years . . . the woman!"

She had seized Mr. Fuller's hand so forcefully I felt embarrassed for her, and tried to persuade the spirit within Ethel to let go, at the same time explaining her true condition to her, gently, but firmly.

After I had explained how she was able to communicate with us, and that the body of the medium was merely a temporary arrangement, the entity calmed down, asking only if he loved her, meaning the other spirit in the house. I assured her that this was so, and then called on Albert, Ethel's spirit guide, to help me ease the troubled one from Ethel's body and thus free her at the same time from the house.

And then the man came into Ethel's body, very emotionally, calling out for Sylvia.

Again I explained how he was able to communicate.

"You see me, don't you." he finally said as he calmed down. "I loved everyone . . . I'll go, I won't bother you . . . "

I called again for Albert, and in a moment his crisp voice replaced the spirit's outcries.

"The man is a Henry MacLellan . . . there stood in this vicinity another house . . . around 1810, 1812 . . . to 1820 . . . a woman connected with this house lies buried here somewhere, and he is looking for her. His daughter . . . Macy? . . . Maisie? About 1798 . . . 16 or 18 years old . . . has been done wrong . . . had to do with a feud of two families . . . McDern . . . ''

Albert then suggested letting the man speak to us directly, and so he did in a little while. I offered my help.

"It is futile," he said. "My problem is my own."

"Who are you?"

"Henry. I lived right here. I was born here."

"What year? What year are we in now as I speak with you?"

"I speak to you in the year 1813."

"Are you a gentleman of some age?"

"I would have forty-seven years."

"Did you serve in any governmental force or agency?"

"My son . . . John Stuart Mc . . . ''

"McDermot? Your son was John Stuart McDermot?"

"You have it from my own lips."

"Where did he serve?"

"Ticonderoga."

And then he added, "My daughter, missing, but I found the bones, buried not too far from here. I am satisfied. I have her with me."

He admitted he knew he was no longer "on the earth plane," but was drawn to the place from time to time.

"But if you ask me as a gentleman to go, I shall go," he added. Under these circumstances — rare ones, indeed, when dealing with hauntings — I suggested he not disturb those in the present house, especially the children. Also, would he not be happier in the world into which he had long passed.

"I shall consider that," he acknowledged, "You speak well, sir.

I have no intention of frightening."

"Are you aware that much time has passed . . . that this is not 1813 any more?" I said.

"I am not aware of this, sir . . . it is always the same time here."

Again I asked if he served in any regiment, but he replied his leg was no good. Was it his land and house? Yes, he replied, he owned it and built the house. But when I pressed him as to where he might be buried, he balked.

"My bones are here with me . . . I am sufficient unto myself."

I then asked about his church affiliation, and he informed me his church was "northeast of here, on Beacon Road." The minister's name was Rooney, but he could not tell me the denomination. His head was not all it used to be.

"A hundred and fifty years have passed," I said, and began the ritual of exorcism. "Go from this house in peace, and with our love."

And so he did.

Albert, Ethel's guide, returned briefly to assure us that all was as it should be and Mr. McDermot was gone from the house; also, that he was being reunited with his mother, Sarah Ann McDermot. And then Albert too withdrew and Ethel returned to her own self again.

I turned to Mrs. Fuller and her cousin, Miss Elliott, for possible comments and corroboration of the information received through Mrs. Meyers in trance.

*   *   *

It appears the house that the Fullers were able to trace back as far as about 1860 was moved to make room for a road, and then set down again not far from that road. Unfortunately going further back proved difficult. I heard again from Mrs. Fuller in December of that year. The footsteps were continuing, it seemed, and her seven-year-old daughter Becky was being frightened by them. She had not yet been able to find any record of Mr. McDermot, but vowed to continue her search.

That was twenty years ago, and nothing further turned up, and I really do not know if the footsteps continued or Mr. McDermot finally gave up his restless quest for a world of which he no longer was a part.

As for Mr. Langdon, whom Ethel Meyers had also identified by name as a presence in the house, he must by now be reunited with his wife Donna, and I hope he has forgiven her her trespasses, as a good Christian might: over there, even her sins do not matter any longer.

A New Hampshire Artist
and Her Ghosts

Elizabeth Nealon Weistrop is a renowned sculptress who lives far away from the mainstream of city life in rural New Hampshire. I talked to her the other day when I had occasion to admire a particularly striking bronze medallion she had created for the Society of Medallists. It was a squirrel such as abound in her New England woods.

Mrs. Weistrop's experiences have given her a sense of living with the uncanny, far from being afraid of it or worried.

"What were the most striking examples of your brush with the uncanny — that is of yourself or your family?" I queried her.

"There are many," Mrs. Weistrop replied, "but I'll try to give you the most evidential incidents. For example, in 1954 when our Debby was six years old, the doctor decided she should be taken out of the first grade and remain at home to recover from nervousness that resulted from a serious infection she had recently recovered from. She missed going to school with her sister Betsy, two years older, but played every day with five-year-old Donna Esdale, a neighbor's little girl.

"Our family, my husband, our two girls, and I, were living in a cottage in West Dennis on Cape Cod at the time and located a better place in Yarmouthport — a warmer house with a studio I could use for sculpture. Donna's father owned a truck, so we paid him to move us to the new house.

"Three weeks later (we had seen no one from West Dennis), Betsy, Debby, and I were eating breakfast and Debby said, 'What happened to Donna?' I said, 'What do you mean?' Debby said, 'Why was Donna's face all covered with blood?' Then Betsy and I explained to Debby that she had just had a bad dream and that Donna was all right, but Debby insisted with questions. 'Did a truck hit her?' 'Did someone hit her in the face?' 'Why was her face all covered with blood?' And no matter how Betsy and I explained about dreams, Debby refused to understand and asked the same questions.

"Finally, the school bus came. Betsy went to school and Debby looked after her wistfully, wanting to go to school too.

"During the day Debby played with her new black puppy, and I was busy working at sculpture, and the breakfast session left my mind.

"About nine o'clock that evening, Donna's father, Ralph, came to the studio and asked how everyone was. I said we were all fine and automatically asked [after] his family. He said, 'All right, except that last night my wife and I were up all night. Donna had nose bleeds all night and her face was just covered with blood!'

"Debby was asleep but Betsy was standing near me, and we turned and stared at each other in wonder.

"While living on Cape Cod in 1956, we rented a house from a Mrs. Ridley in West Hyannisport. The house she rented to us had belonged to her mother, a woman in her eighties who had recently died. Mrs. Ridley lived next door with her husband and a daughter, Rodella. I found them pleasant people, proud of their American Indian ancestry and sadly missing the grandmother fondly referred to as 'Gunny.' They spoke of her so often and of her constant activity making repairs on the home she loved that I almost felt I knew her. When they told me of their own supernatural experiences, they did not find a skeptic in me, as my own mother whom I had loved dearly had been gifted with ESP. My mother had been the old child born with a caul [veil] in an Irish family of eleven children, and as I grew up I became very familiar with my mother's amazing and correct predictions. My own experiences with the unknown had been limited to a strong feeling of a force or power leading and directing me in my work as a sculptor.

"One sunny fall afternoon, I was alone concentrating on a sculpture of St. Francis. My husband, Harry, was away for the day and our two girls were in school, when I heard a loud thump from the bedroom which our girls shared. This room had been the large sunny bedroom of 'Gunny' and within easy view of where I was working. I stopped work to investigate, expecting to see that a large piece of furniture had collapsed or been overturned. As I searched the room and looked out of the window, I could discover nothing that could have made such a sound. Still puzzled, I walked into the next room, the kitchen, and noted that our highly nervous dog was sleeping soundly — a dog who was always on her feet barking at the slightest sound. The clock in the kitchen said 2:30 and that would give me one half hour more to concentrate on St. Francis, so I went back to work, still wondering.

"That evening after the girls were asleep I walked outside in back of the house, and Mrs. Ridley, who was sitting on her back porch, invited me into her house to have coffee with her, her daughter, and her daughter's fiance.

"While we chatted around the table, Mrs. Ridley told of sitting by her kitchen window that afternoon and having *seen her mother,* 'Gunny,' *just as clear as day, walk up the path from the woods* to our house and go over and knock on her own bedroom window at our house.

"I asked, 'What time was that?' and Mrs. Ridley answered, 'At 2:30.' "

John, up in Vermont

This isn't exactly a ghost story, if ghosts are troubled individuals unaware of their passing and status, with some sort of compulsion unresolved. But then again, it is, if you consider the afterlife full of fine distinctions as to who is a ghost and who is simply a troubled spirit.

Not far from Stowe, Vermont, in what I have long thought of as the most beautiful part of New England, there is a country house that once belonged to the late lyricist John LaTouche. He and a friend, who shall remain nameless, co-owned the place, I believe, and for all I know, the friend still does. But John hasn't really left entirely either. He is buried up there in Vermont in a flower bed, amid his favorite trees and hills. That is, his body is. As for the rest, well now, that is another matter entirely.

I first met John LaTouche through the late medium and psychic investigator Eileen Garrett over lunch at the Hotel St. Regis in New York. She thought, and rightly so, that we would become friends since we had in common not only our professional pursuits — I, too, am a lyricist, among other professional aspects — but also our intense involvement with the paranormal. Soon after this initial meeting, John invited me to a private dinner party at his home on East 55th Street, right across from an ancient firehouse, where he occupied the magnificent penthouse — at the time he was doing well financially (which was not always the case) because his "Ballad for Americans" and the musical *The Legend of Baby Doe* were paying him handsomely.

With the party was also my late friend and medium Ethel Johnson Meyers and the actress Future Fulton, who was very psychic, and the four of us held a seance after dinner.

Picture my surprise when it was John who went under first, showing he had trance abilities also. Regrettably, I do not have an exact transcript of what came through him at that time, but it seemed that a distant ancestor of his, a Breton lady, wanted to manifest and reassure him in his work and quest for success. No sooner had he returned to his normal state, than Ethel described in great detail what the spirit looked like, and considering that Ethel would not have known the details of an eighteenth century Breton woman's costume, this seemed rather interesting to me at the time.

Sometimes, when people with psychic gifts link up, the mediumship goes back and forth as the case may require. Several months after this initial get-together, I was in rehearsal with a musical revue, my first theatrical involvement, in which Future Fulton had a singing role. I had made an appointment with John to see him the Friday of that week. "Are you fry Freeday?" I asked, "I mean, are you free Friday?" We set a meeting for three o'clock. Unfortunately, it slipped my mind in the heat of rehearsals until about 2 on Friday. It became impossible for me to break away from the goings-on and get to a phone, and I had visions of John never wanting to speak to me again for having stood him up. When Future noticed my distress, she inquired as to its cause, and when I told her, she said, "Oh well, that's nothing. I will get through to John."

With that she sat down on a bench, leaned back, closed her eyes for a moment, and then said cheerfully, "It is done. Don't worry about it."

Being forever the scientific investigator, I was not really relieved. As soon as I could, at around seven o'clock. I rushed to the nearest telephone and called John. Before he could say a word, I began to apologize profusely for the missed appointment, and my inability to notify him.

"What are you babbling about?" John interjected, when I caught my breath for a moment. "Of course you called me."

"I did not."

"No? Then why is there a message on my tape machine from you telling me you could not make it?"

"There is?"

"Yes . . . must have been around two or so because I got back in time for our meeting a little after that, and it was on the tape."

I did not know what to say. Later, I told John, who just shook his head and smiled.

Time went on, and we met now and again, usually at his house. On one occasion, we were invited for a run-through of a new work he and his friend with whom he shared the house in Vermont had written. John seemed in the best of health and creative activity.

It was in August of 1956, and I had just come home from the opening night of my play *Hotel Excelsior,* a less than brilliant piece of mine at the Provincetown Theatre in Greenwich Village, and I checked my answering service as was my custom.

"Only one message," the operator said laconically. "John LaTouche has died."

I was in a state of shock. But as I found out, John had gone to his Vermont retreat that weekend and nothing had been wrong. Now John was overweight, and he liked to eat well. Apparently too

Ghosts of New England

well, for after a heavy meal he had had a heart attack and died. Or rather, his body gave out.

For it was not the end of our friendship by a long shot. I did not attend the funeral up in Vermont, which was for close family only. His mother Effy did, and Effy and I were friendly for a while after, until she too passed into the Great Beyond.

Maybe three or four months passed.

Ethel Meyers and I were doing a routine investigation of a haunted house somewhere in Connecticut. Picture my surprise when she suddenly went into trance, and the next voice I heard was not some obscure ghostly person stuck in that particular house for whatever personal reasons, but my old friend John LaTouche!

"Greetings, Hans," he said in almost his usual voice, and then went on to explain how touched he was by his funeral amid the flowers up in Vermont. But he was not there. Not John.

Since that time, John has communicated with me now and again, telling me that he has adjusted to his sudden departure from the physical world — he was only 39 at the time of his death — and that he was still creating works of art for the stage, Over There.

Then, too, he became sort of an adviser to me, especially in matters theatrical, and he began to use not only Ethel Meyers as his channel, but also others.

I don't know when the celestial Board of Directors will want to send John back to earth in his next incarnation, but for the moment at least, he seems to be a free spirit doing his thing, communicating hither and yon, apparently able to drop in, so to speak, at seances and investigations, at will. The only place I am sure he is not at, is up in Vermont under the flowers.

The Ghosts of Stamford Hill

"**M**r. Holzer," the voice on the phone said pleasantly, "I've read your book and that's why I'm calling. We've got a ghost in our house."

Far from astonished, I took paper and pencil and, not unlike a grocery-store clerk taking down a telephone order, started to put down the details of the report.

Robert Cowan is a gentleman with a very balanced approach to life. He is an artist who works for one of the leading advertising agencies in New York City and his interests range widely from art to music, theater, history, and what have you. But not to ghosts, at least not until he and his actress-wife, Dorothy, moved into the 1780 House on Stamford Hill. The house is thus named for the simplest of all reasons: it was built in that year.

Mr. Cowan explained that he thought I'd be glad to have a look at his house, although the Cowans were not unduly worried about the presence of a nonrent-paying guest at their house. Although it was a bit disconcerting at times, it was curiosity as to what the ghost wanted and who the specter was that had prompted Bob Cowan to seek the help of The Ghost Hunter.

I said, "Mr. Cowan, would you mind putting your experiences

in writing, so I can have them for my files?" I like to have written reports (in the first person, if possible) so that later I can refer back to them if similar cases should pop up, as they often do.

"Not at all," Bob Cowan said. "I'll be glad to write it down for you."

The next morning I received his report, along with a brief history of the 1780 House.

Here is a brief account of the experiences my wife and I have had while living in this house during the past nine and a half years. I'll start with myself because my experiences are quite simple.

From time to time (once a week or so) during most of the time we've lived here I have noticed unidentifiable movements out of the corner of my eye . . . day or night. Most often, I've noticed this while sitting in our parlor and what I see moving seems to be in the livingroom. At other times, and only late at night when I am the only one awake, I hear beautiful but unidentified music seemingly played by a full orchestra, as though a radio were on in another part of the house.

The only place I recall hearing this is in an upstairs bedroom and just after I've gone to bed. Once I actually got up, opened the bedroom door to ascertain if it was perhaps music from a radio accidentally left on, but it wasn't.

Finally, quite often I've heard a variety of knocks and crashes that do not have any logical source within the structural setup of the house. A very loud smash occurred two weeks ago. You'd have thought a door had fallen off its hinges upstairs but, as usual, there was nothing out of order.

My wife, Dorothy, had two very vivid experiences about five years ago. One was in the kitchen, or rather outside of a kitchen window. She was standing at the sink in the evening and happened to glance out the window when she saw a face glaring in at her. It was a dark face but not a Negro, perhaps Indian; it was very hateful and fierce.

At first she thought it was a distorted reflection in the glass but in looking closer, it was a face glaring directly at her. All she could make out was a face only and as she recalls it, *it seemed translucent*. It didn't disappear, *she did!*

On a summer afternoon my wife was taking a nap in a back bedroom and was between being awake and being asleep when she heard the sounds of men's voices and the sound of working on the grounds — rakes, and garden tools — right outside of the window. She tried to arouse herself to see who they could be, but she couldn't get up.

At that time, and up to that time we had only hired a single man to come in and work on the lawn and flower beds. It wasn't until at least a year later that we hired a crew that came in and worked once a week, and we've often wondered if this was an experience of precognition. My wife has always had an uneasy feeling about the outside of the back of the house and still sometimes hears men's voices outside and will look out all windows without seeing anyone.

She also has shared my experiences of seeing "things" out of the corner of her eye and also hearing quite lovely music at night. She hasn't paid attention to household noises because a long time ago I told her "all old houses have odd structural noises" . . . which is true enough.

Prior to our living here the house was lived in for about 25 years by the Clayton Rich family, a family of five. Mr. Rich died towards the end of their stay here. By the time we bought it, the three children were all married and had moved away.

For perhaps one year prior to that a Mrs. David Cowles lived here. She's responsible for most of the restoration along with a Mr. Frederick Kinble.

Up until 1927 or 1928 the house was in the Weed family ever since 1780. The last of the line were two sisters who hated each other and only communicated with each other through the husband of one of the sisters. They had divided the house and used two different doors. One used the regular front door into the stair hall and the other used the "coffin door" into the parlor.

Mr. Cowan added that they were selling the house — not because of ghosts but because they wanted to move to the city again. I assured him that we'd be coming up as soon as possible.

Before we could make arrangements to do so, I had another note from the Cowans. On February 9, 1964, Bob Cowan wrote that they heard a singing voice quite clearly downstairs, and music again.

It wasn't until the following week, however, that my wife and I went to Stamford Hill. The Cowans offered to have supper ready for us that Sunday evening and to pick us up at the station since nobody could find the house at night who did not know the way.

It was around six o'clock in the evening when our New Haven train pulled in. Bob Cowan wore the Scottish beret he had said he would wear in order to be recognized by us at once. The house stands at the end of a winding road that runs for about ten minutes through woodland and past shady lanes. An American eagle over the door, and the date 1780, stood out quite clearly despite the dusk that had started to settle on the land. The house has three levels, and the Cowans used the large room next to the kitchen in what might be called the cellar or ground level for their dining room.

They had adorned it with eighteenth-century American antiques in a most winning manner, and the fireplace added a warmth to the room, making it seem miles removed from bustling New York.

On the next level were the livingroom and next to that a kind of sitting room. The fireplace in each of these rooms connected one to the other. Beyond the corridor there was the master bedroom and Bob's colorful den. Upstairs were two guest rooms, and there was a small attic accessible only through a hole in the ceiling and by ladder. Built during the American Revolution, the house stands on a wooded slope, which is responsible for its original name of Woodpecker Ridge Farm.

Many years ago, after the restoration of the house was completed, Harold Donaldson Eberlin, an English furniture and garden expert, wrote about it:

> With its rock-ribbed ridges, it boulder-strewn pastures and its sharply broken contours like the choppy surface of a wind-blown sea, the topographical conditions have inevitably affected the domestic architecture. To mention only two particulars, the dwellings of the region have had to accommodate themselves to many an abrupt hillside site and the employment of some of the omnipresent granite boulders. Part of the individuality of the house at Woodpecker Ridge Farm lies in the way it satisfies these conditions without being a type house.
>
> Before communal existence, the country all thereabouts bore the pleasantly descriptive name of Woodpecker Ridge, and Woodpecker Ridge Farm was so called in order to keep alive the memory of this early name. Tradition says that the acres now comprised within the boundaries of Woodpecker Ridge Farm once formed part of the private hunting ground of *the old Indian chief Ponus*.

Old Ponus may, perhaps, appear a trifle mythical and shadowy, as such long-gone chieftains are wont to be. Very substantial and real, however, was Augustus Weed, who built the house in 1780. And the said Augustus was something of a personage.

War clouds were still hanging thick over the face of the land when he had the foundation laid and the structure framed. Nevertheless, confident and forward-looking, he not only reared a staunch and tidy abode, indicative of the spirit of the countryside, but he seems to have put into it some of his own robust and independent personality as well.

It is said that Augustus was such a notable farmer and took such justifiable pride in the condition of his fields that he was not afraid to make a standing offer of one dollar reward for every daisy that anyone could find in his hay.

About 1825 the house experienced a measure of remodeling in accordance with the notions prevalent at the time. Nothing very extensive or ostentatious was attempted, but visible traces of the work then undertaken remain in the neo-Greek details that occur both outside and indoors.

It is not at all unlikely that the "lie-on-your-stomach" windows of the attic story date from this time and point to either a raising of the original roof or else some alteration of its pitch. These "lie-on-your-stomach" windows — so called because they were low down in the wall and had their sills very near the level of the floor so that you had almost to lie on your stomach to look out of them — were a favorite device of the *neo-Grec* era for lighting attic rooms. And it is remarkable how much light they actually do give, and what a pleasant light it is.

The recent remodeling that brought Woodpecker

Farmhouse to its present state of comeliness and comfort impaired none of the individual character the place had acquired through the generations that had passed since hardy Augustus Weed first took up his abode there. It needs no searching scrutiny to discern the eighteenth-century features impressed on the structure at the beginning — the stout timbers of the framing, the sturdy beams and joists, the wide floor boards, and the generous fireplaces. Neither is close examination required to discover the marks of the 1825 rejuvenation.

The fashions of columns, pilasters, mantelpieces, and other features speak plainly and proclaim their origin.

The aspect of the garden, too, discloses the same sympathetic understanding of the environment peculiarly suitable to the sort of house for which it affords the natural setting. The ancient well cover, the lilac bushes, the sweet-briers, the August lilies, and the other denizens of an old farmhouse dooryard have been allowed to keep their long-accustomed places.

In return for this recognition of their prescriptive rights, they lend no small part to the air of self-possessed assurance and mellow contentment that pervades the whole place.

After a most pleasant dinner downstairs, Catherine and I joined the Cowans in the large livingroom upstairs. We sat down quietly and hoped we would hear something along musical lines.

As the quietness of the countryside slowly settled over us, I could indeed distinguish faraway, indistinct musical sounds, as if someone were playing a radio underwater or at great distance. A check revealed no nearby house or parked car whose radio could be responsible for this.

After a while we got up and looked about the room itself. We were standing about quietly admiring the furniture when both my wife and I and, of course, the Cowans, clearly heard footsteps overhead.

They were firm and strong and could not be mistaken for anything else, such as a squirrel in the attic or other innocuous noises. Nor was it an old house settling.

"Did you hear that?" I said, almost superfluously.

"We all heard it," my wife said and looked at me.

"What am I waiting for?" I replied, and faster than you can say Ghost Hunter, I was up the stairs and into the room above our heads where the steps had been heard. The room lay in total darkness. I turned the switch. There was no one about. Nobody else was in the house at the time, and all windows were closed. We decided to assemble upstairs in the smaller room next to the one in which I had heard the steps. The reason was that Mrs. Cowan had experienced a most unusual phenomenon in that particular room.

"It was like lightning," she said, "a bright light suddenly come and gone."

I looked the room over carefully. The windows were arranged in such a manner that a reflection from passing cars was out of the question. Both windows, far apart and on different walls, opened into the dark countryside away from the only road.

Catherine and I sat down on the couch, and the Cowans took chairs. We sat quietly for perhaps twenty minutes without lights, except a small amount of light filtering in from the stairwell. It was very dark, certainly dark enough for sleep, and there was not light enough to write by.

As I was gazing toward the back wall of the little room and wondering about the footsteps I had just heard so clearly, I saw a blinding flash of light, white light, in the corner facing me. It came on and disappeared very quickly, so quickly in fact that my wife, whose head had been turned in another direction at the moment, missed it. But Dorothy Cowan saw it and exclaimed, "There it is again. Exactly as I saw it."

Despite its brevity I was able to observe that the light cast a shadow on the opposite wall, so it could not very well have been a hallucination.

I decided it would be best to bring Mrs. Meyers to the house, and we went back to New York soon after. While we were preparing our return visit with Mrs. Meyers as our medium, I received an urgent call from Bob Cowan.

"Since seeing you and Cathy at our house, we've had some additional activity that you'll be interested in. Dottie and I have both heard knocking about the house but none of it in direct answer to questions that we've tried to ask. On Saturday, the twenty-ninth of February, I was taking a nap back in my studio when I was awakened by the sound of footsteps in the room above me . . . the same room we all sat in on the previous Sunday.

"The most interesting event was on the evening of Thursday, February 27. I was driving home from the railroad station alone. Dottie was still in New York. As I approached the house, I noticed that there was a light on in the main floor bedroom and also a light on up in the sewing room on the top floor, a room Dottie also uses for rehearsal. I thought Dottie had left the lights on. I drove past the house and down to the garage, put the car away and then walked back to the house and noticed that the light in the top floor was now off.

"I entered the house and noticed that the dogs were calm (wild enough at seeing me, but in no way indicating that there was anyone else in the house). I went upstairs and found that the light in the bedroom was also off. I checked the entire house and there was absolutely no sign that anyone had been there . . . and there hadn't been, I'm sure."

* * *

On Sunday, March 15, we arrived at the 1780 House, again at dusk. A delicious meal awaited us downstairs, then we repaired to the upstairs part of the house.

We seated ourselves in the large livingroom where the music had been heard, and where we had been standing at the time we heard the uncanny footsteps overhead.

"I sense a woman in a white dress," Ethel said suddenly. "She's got dark hair and a high forehead. Rather a small woman."

"I was looking through the attic earlier," Bob Cowan said thoughtfully, "and look what I found — a waistcoat that would fit a rather smallish woman or girl."

The piece of clothing he showed us seemed rather musty. There were a number of articles up there in the attic that must have belonged to an earlier owner of the house — much earlier.

A moment later, Ethel Meyers showed the characteristic signs of onsetting trance. We doused the lights until only one back light was on.

At first, only inarticulate sounds came from the medium's lips. "You can speak," I said, to encourage her. "You're among friends." The sounds now turned into crying.

"What is your name?" I asked, as I always do on such occasions. There was laughter — whether girlish or mad was hard to tell.

Suddenly, she started to sing in a high-pitched voice.

"You can speak, you can speak," I kept assuring the entity. Finally she seemed to have settled down somewhat in control of the medium.

"Happy to speak with you," she mumbled faintly.

"What is your name?"

I had to ask it several times before I could catch the answer clearly.

"Lucy."

"Tell me, Lucy, do you live here?"

"God be with you."

"Do you live in this house?"

"My house."

"What year is this?"

The entity hesitated a moment, then turned toward Dorothy and said, "I like you."

I continued to question her.

"How old are you?"

"Old lady."

"How old?"

"God be with you."

The conversation had been friendly until I asked her, "What is your husband's name?" The ghost drew back as if I had spoken a horrible word.

"What did you say?" she almost shouted, her voice trembling with emotion. "I have no husband — God bless you — what were you saying?" she repeated, then started to cry again. "Husband, husband," she kept saying as if it was a thought she could not bear.

"You did not have a husband, then?"

"Yes, I did."

"Your name again?"

"Lucy . . . fair day . . . where is he? The fair day . . . the pretty one, he said to me look in the pool, and you will see my face."

"Who is he?" I asked.

But the ghost paid no heed to me. She was evidently caught up in her own memories.

"I heard a voice, Lucy, Lucy . . . fair one . . . alack . . . they took him out . . . they laid him cold in the ground . . . ."

"What year was that?" I wanted to know.

"Year, year?" she repeated. "Now, *now!*"

"Who rules this country now?"

"Why, he who seized it."

"Who rules?"

"They carried him out . . . the Savior of our country. General Washington."

"When did he die?"

"Just now."

I tried to question her further, but she returned to the thoughts of her husband.

"I want to stay here . . . I wait at the pool . . . look, he is there!" She was growing excited again.

"I want to stay here now, always, forever . . . rest in peace . . . he is there always with me."

"How long ago did you die?" I asked, almost casually. The reaction was somewhat hostile.

"I have not died . . . never . . . All Saints!"

I asked her to join her loved one by calling for him and thus be set free of this house. But the ghost would have none of it.

"Gainsay what I have spoke . . . "

"How did you come to this house?" I now asked.

"Father . . . I am born here."

"Was it your father's house?"

"Yes."

"What was his name?" I asked, but the restless spirit of Lucy was slipping away now, and Albert, the medium's control, took over. His crisp, clear voice told us that the time had come to release Ethel.

"What about this woman, Lucy?" I inquired. Sometimes the control will give additional details.

"He was not her husband . . . he was killed before she married him," Albert said.

No wonder my question about a husband threw Lucy into an uproar of emotions.

In a little while, Ethel Meyers was back to her old self, and as usual, did not remember anything of what had come through her entranced lips.

Shortly after this episode my wife and I went to Europe.

* * *

As soon as we returned, I called Bob Cowan. How were things up in Stamford Hill? Quiet? Not very.

"Last June," Bob recalled, "Dottie and I were at home with a friend, a lady hair dresser, who happens to be psychic. We were playing around with the Ouija board, more in amusement than seriously. Suddenly, the Sunday afternoon quiet was disrupted by heavy footsteps coming up the steps outside the house. Quickly, we hid the Ouija board, for we did not want a potential buyer of the house to see us in this unusual pursuit. We were sure someone was coming up to see the house. But the steps stopped abruptly when they reached the front door. I opened [it], and there was no one outside."

"Hard to sell a house that way," I commented. "Anything else?"

"Yes, in July we had a house guest, a very balanced person, not given to imagining things. There was a sudden crash upstairs, and when I rushed up the stairs to the sewing room, there was this bolt of material that had been standing in a corner, lying in the middle of the room as if thrown there by unseen hands! Margaret, our house guest, also heard someone humming a tune in the bathroom, although there was no one in there at the time. Then in November, when just the two of us were in the house, someone knocked at the door downstairs. Again we looked, but there was nobody outside. One evening when I was in the 'ship' room and Dottie in the bedroom, we heard footfalls coming down the staircase.

"Since neither of us was causing them and the door was closed, only a ghost could have been walking down those stairs."

"But the most frightening experience of all," Dorothy Cowan

broke in, "was when I was sleeping downstairs and, waking up, wanted to go to the bathroom without turning on the lights, so as not to wake Bob. Groping my way back to bed, I suddenly found myself up on the next floor in the blue room, which is pretty tricky walking in the dark. I had the feeling someone was forcing me to follow them into that particular room."

I had heard enough, and on December 15, we took Ethel Johnson Meyers to the house for another go at the restless ones within its confines. Soon we were all seated in the ship room on the first floor, and Ethel started to drift into a trance.

"There is a baby's coffin here," she murmured. "Like a newborn infant's."

The old grandfather clock in back of us kept ticking away loudly.

"I hear someone call Maggie," Ethel said. "Margaret."

"Do you see anyone?"

"A woman, about five foot two, in a long dress, with a big bustle in the back. Hair down, parted in the middle, and braided on both sides. There is another young woman . . . Laurie . . . very pretty face, but so sad . . . she's looking at you, Hans . . . "

"What is it she wants?" I asked quietly.

"A youngish man with brown hair, curly, wearing a white blouse, taken in at the wrists, and over it a tan waistcoat, but no coat over it . . . "

I asked what he wanted and why he was here. This seemed to agitate the medium somewhat.

"Bottom of the well," she mumbled, "stone at bottom of the well."

Bob Cowan changed seats, moving away from the coffin door to the opposite side of the room. He complained of feeling cold at the former spot, although neither door nor window was open to cause such a sensation.

"Somebody had a stick over his shoulder," the medium said now, "older man wearing dark trousers, heavy stockings. His hair is gray and kind of longish; he's got that stick."

I asked her to find out why.

"Take him away," Ethel replied. "He says, 'Take him away!'"

"But he was innocent, he went to the well. Who is down in the well? Him who I drove into the well, him . . . I mistook . . . "

Ethel was now fully entranced, and the old man seemed to be speaking through her.

"What is your name?" I asked.

"She was agrievin'," the voice replied, "she were grievin' I did that."

"What is your name?"

"Ain't no business to you."

"How can I help you?"

"They're all here . . . accusin' me . . . I see her always by the well."

"Did someone die in this well?" Outside, barely twenty yards away, was the well, now cold and silent in the night air.

"Him who I mistook. I find peace, I find him, I put him together again."

"What year was that?"

"No matter to you now . . . I do not forgive myself . . . I wronged, I wronged . . . I see always her face look on me."

"Are you in this house now?" I asked.

"Where else can I be and talk with thee?" the ghost shot back.

"This isn't your house anymore," I said quietly.

"Oh, yes it is," the ghost replied firmly. "The young man stays here only to look upon me and mock me. It will not be other than mine. I care only for that flesh that I could put again on the bone, and I will restore him to the bloom of life and the rich love of her who suffered through my own misdemeanor."

"Is your daughter buried here?" I asked, to change the subject. Quietly, the ghostly voice said, "Yes."

But he refused to say where he himself was laid to final — or not so final — rest.

At this point the ghost realized that he was not in his own body, and as I explained the procedure to him, he gradually became calmer. At first, he thought he was in his own body and could use it to restore to life the one he had slain. I kept asking him who he was. Finally, in a soft whisper, came the reply, "Samuel."

"And Laurie?"

"My daughter . . . oh, he is here, the man I wronged . . . Margaret, Margaret!" He seemed greatly agitated with fear now.

The big clock started to strike. The ghost somehow felt it meant him.

"The judgment, the judgment . . . Laurie . . . they smile at me. I have killed. He has taken my hand! He whom I have hurt."

But the excitement proved too much for Samuel. Suddenly, he was gone, and after a brief interval, an entirely different personality inhabited Ethel's body. It was Laurie.

"Please forgive him," she pleaded. "I have forgiven him."

The voice was sweet and girlish.

"Who is Samuel?"

"My grandfather."

"What is your family name"

"Laurie Ho-Ho- . . . if I could only get that name."

But she couldn't.

Neither could she give me the name of her beloved, killed by her grandfather. It was a name she was not allowed to mention around the house, so she had difficulty remembering now, she explained.

"What is your mother's name?" I asked.

"Margaret."

"What year were you born?"

Hesitatingly, the voice said, "Seventeen-fifty-six."

"What year is this now?"

"Seventeen seventy-four. We laid him to rest in seventeen seventy-four."

"In the church?"

"No, Grandfather could not bear it. We laid him to rest on the hill to the north. We dug with our fingers all night. Didn't tell Grandpa where we put it."

"How far from here is it?"

"No more than a straight fly of the lark."

"Is the grave marked?"

"Oh, no."

"What happened to your father?"

"No longer home, gone."

I explained to Laurie that the house would soon change hands, and that she must not interfere with this. The Cowans had the feeling that their ghosts were somehow keeping all buyers away, fantastic though this may be at first thought. But then all of psychic research is pretty unusual and who is to say what cannot be?

Laurie promised not to interfere and to accept a new owner of "their" house. She left, asking again that her grandfather be forgiven his sins.

I then asked Albert, Ethel's control, to take over the medium. That done, I queried him regarding the whole matter.

"The father is buried far from here, but most of the others are buried around here," he said. "During the year seventeen seventy-seven . . . Grandfather was not brought here until later when there was forgiveness. The body was removed and put in Christian burial."

"Where is the tombstone?" I asked.

"Lying to the west of a white structure," Albert replied in his precise slightly accented speech, "on these grounds. The tombstone is broken off, close to the earth. The top has been mishandled by vandals. The old man is gone, the young man has taken him by the hand."

"What was the young man's name?"

"She called him Benjamin."

"He was killed in the well?"

"That is right. He has no grave except on the hill."

"Is the old man the one who disturbs this house?"

"He is the main one who brings in his rabble, looking for the young man."

"Who is Lucy?" I asked, referring back to the girl who had spoken to us at the last seance in the late spring.

"That is the girl you were talking about, Laurie. Her name is really Lucy. One and the same person."

"She was not actually married to the young man?"

"In her own way, she was. But they would not recognize it. There were differences in religious ideas. . . . But we had better release the medium for now."

I nodded, and within a moment or two, Ethel was back to herself, very much bewildered as to what went on while she was in trance.

"How do you reconcile these dates with the tradition that this house was built in seventeen eighty?" I asked Bob Cowan.

He shook his head.

"It is only a tradition. We have no proof of the actual date."

We went to the upstairs sewing room where the latest manifestations had taken place, and grouped ourselves around the heavy wooden table. Ethel almost immediately fell into trance again. She rarely does twice in one sitting.

The voice reverberating in the near darkness now was clearly that of a man, and a very dominating voice it was.

"Who are you?" I demanded.

"Sergeant-major . . . . " No name followed. I asked why was he here in this house.

"One has pleasant memories."

"Your name?"

"Sergeant-major Harm."

"First name?"

Instead of giving it, he explained that he once owned the house and was "friend, not foe." I looked at Bob Cowan, who knows all the owners of the property in the old records, and Bob shook his head. No Harm.

"When I please, I come. I do not disturb willingly. But I will go," the new visitor offered. "I will take him with me; you will see him no more. I am at peace with him now. He is at peace with me."

"How did you pass over?" I inquired.

"On the field of battle. On the banks of the Potomac . . . seventeen seventy-six."

"What regiment were you in?" I continued.

"York . . . Eight . . . I was foot soldier . . . eighteenth regiment . . . "

"What army?"

"Wayne . . . Wayne . . . "

"Who was your commanding general?"

"Broderick."

"Who was the colonel of your regiment?"

"Wayne, Wayne."

"You were a sergeant-major?"

"Sergeant-major, eighteenth regiment, foot infantry."

"Where were you stationed?"

"New York."

"Where in New York?"

"Champlain."

"Your regimental commander again?"

"Broderick." Then he added, not without emotion, "I died under fire, first battle of Potomac."

"Where are you buried?"

"Fort Ticonderoga, New York."

I wondered how a soldier fighting on the banks of the Potomac could be buried in upstate New York. But I must confess that the word "Potomac" had come so softly that I could have been mistaken.

"The date of your death?"

"Seventeen seventy-six."

Then he added, as the voice became more and more indistinct, "I will leave now, but I will protect you from those who . . . who are hungry to . . . " The voice trailed off into silence.

A few moments later, Ethel emerged from the trance with a slight headache, but otherwise her old self. As usual, she did not recall anything that had come through her entranced lips.

* * *

We returned to New York soon after, hoping that all would remain quiet in the Cowan house, and, more important, that there would soon be a new laird of the manor at the 1780 House.

I, too, heard the ghostly music, although I am sure it does not connect with the colonial ghosts we were able to evoke. The music I heard sounded like a far-off radio, which it wasn't since there are no houses near enough to be heard from. What I heard for a few moments in the livingroom sounded like a full symphony orchestra playing the music popular around the turn of this century.

Old houses impregnated with layers upon layers of people's emotions frequently also absorb music and other sounds as part of the atmosphere.

What about the sergeant-major?

I checked the regimental records. No soldier named Harm, but a number of officers (and men) named Harmon. I rechecked my tapes. The name "Harm" had been given by the ghost very quietly. He could have said Harmon. Or perhaps he was disguising his identity as they sometimes will.

But then I discovered something very interesting. In the Connecticut state papers there is mention of a certain Benjamin Harmon, Jr., Lt., who was with a local regiment in 1776. The murdered young man had been identified as "Benjamin." Suddenly we have another ghost named Harm or Harmon, evidently an older personality. Was he the father of the murdered young man?

The 1780 House is, of course, recorded as dating back to 1780 only. But could not another building have occupied the area? Was the 1780 House an adaptation of a smaller dwelling of which there is no written record?

We can neither prove nor disprove this.

It is true, however, that General "Mad" Anthony Wayne was in charge of the revolutionary troops in the New York area at the time under discussion.

At any rate, all this is knowledge not usually possessed by a lady voice teacher, which is what Ethel Meyers was when not being a medium.

Two years after our visit, the local archaeological society asked for permission to dig around the property since some interesting artifacts had been found on the grounds of the house next door. Picture their — and everyone's — surprise when they found, near a dried up well on the Cowan property, two partly damaged tombstones inscribed "Samuel" and "Benjamin." The stones and the inscriptions were of the late eighteenth century.

The house later changed hands and the Cowans moved to Georgia. I have not heard anything further about any disturbances at the 1780 House, nor do I frankly expect any: Over There Samuel and Benjamin must have made up long ago, and perhaps even have had a go at it again for another round of incarnation, somewhere, some place, some time.

The Haunted Organ at Yale

Yale University in New Haven, Connecticut, is an austere and respectable institution, which does not take such matters as ghostly manifestations very lightly. I must, therefore, keep the identity of my informant a secret, but anyone who wishes to visit Yale and admire its magnificent, historical organ is, of course, at liberty to do so, provided he or she gets clearance from the proper authorities. I would suggest, however, that the matter of ghostly goings-on not be mentioned at such a time. If you happen to experience something out of the ordinary while visiting the organ, well and good, but let it not be given as the reason to the university authorities for your intended visit.

I first heard about this unusual organ in 1969 when a gentleman who was then employed as an assistant organist at Yale had been asked to look after the condition and possible repairs of the huge organ, a very large instrument located in Woolsey Hall. This is the fifth largest organ in the world and has a most interesting history.

Woolsey Hall was built as part of a complex of three buildings for Yale's two-hundredth anniversary in 1901 by the celebrated architects, Carere and Hastings. Shortly after its completion the then university organist, Mr. Harry B. Jepson, succeeded in getting the Newberry family, of the famous department store clan, to contribute a large sum of money for a truly noble organ to be built for the hall.

Even in 1903 it was considered to be an outstanding instrument because of its size and range. By 1915, certain advances in the technology of pipe organs made the 1903 instruments somewhat old fashioned. Again Jepson contacted the Newberry family about the possibility of updating their gift so that the organ could be rebuilt and the hall enlarged. This new instrument was then dedicated in 1916 or thereabouts.

By 1926 musical tastes had again shifted toward romantic music, and it became necessary to make certain additions to the stops as well as the basic building blocks of the classical ensemble. Once again the Newberry family contributed toward the updating of the instrument. The alterations were undertaken by the Skinner Organ Company of Boston, in conjunction with an English expert by the name of G. Donald Harrison. Skinner and Harrison did not get on well together and much tension was present when they restored and brought the venerable old organ up-to-date.

Professor Harry Jepson was forced to retire in the 1940s, against his wishes, and though he lived down the street only two blocks from Woolsey Hall, he never again set foot into it to play the famous organ that he had caused to be built. He died a bitter and disappointed man sometime in 1952.

The last university organist, Frank Bozyan, retired in the 1970s, with great misgivings. He confided to someone employed by the hall that he felt he was making a mistake; within six months after his retirement he was dead. As time went on, Woolsey Hall, once a temple of beauty for the fine arts, was being used for rock and roll groups and mechanically amplified music. Undoubtedly, those connected with the building of the hall and the organ would have been horrified at the goings-on had they been able to witness them.

The gentleman who brought all of this to my attention, and who shall remain nameless, had occasion to be in the hall and involved with the organ itself frequently. He became aware of a menacing and melancholic sensation in the entire building, particularly in the basement and the organ chambers. While working there at odd hours late at night, he became acutely aware of some sort of unpleasant sensation just lurking around the next corner or even standing behind him! On many occasions he found it necessary to look behind him in order to make sure he was alone. The feeling of a presence became so strong he refused to be there by himself, especially in the evenings. Allegedly, the wife of one of the curators advised him to bring a crucifix whenever he had occasion to go down to the organ chambers. She also claimed to have felt someone standing at the entrance door to the basement, as if to keep strangers out.

I visited Yale and the organ one fine summer evening in the company of my informant, who has since found employment elsewhere. I, too, felt the oppressive air in the organ chambers, the sense of a presence whenever I moved about. Whether we are dealing here with the ghost of the unhappy man who was forced to retire and who never set foot again into his beloved organ chamber, or whether we are dealing with an earlier influence, is hard to say. Not for a minute do I suggest that Yale University is haunted or that there are any evil influences concerning the university itself. But it is just possible that sensitive individuals visiting the magnificent organ at Woolsey Hall might pick up some remnant of an unresolved past.

The Terror on the Farm

Notify Woodstock, Connecticut, is New England at its best and quietest: rolling farmland seldom interrupted by the incursions of factories and modern city life.

The village itself seems to have weathered the passage of time rather well and with a minimum of change. Except for the inevitable store signs and other expressions of contemporary American bad taste, the village is as quiet today as it must have been, say, two hundred years ago, when America was young.

On Brickyard Road, going toward the outer edges of the village and standing somewhat apart from the inhabited areas, is an old farmhouse. At the time this incident takes place, it had obviously seen better days; it was totally dilapidated and practically beyond repair. Still, it was a house of some size and quite obviously different from the ordinary small farmhouses of the surrounding countryside.

For the past fifty years, the sixteen-room house, had been the property of the Duprey family. The house itself was built in pre-revolutionary times by the Lyons family, who used it as a tavern. The place was a busy spot on the Boston-Hartford road, and a tavern here did well indeed in the days when railroads had not yet come into existence.

After the Lyons Tavern changed hands, it belonged successfully to the Potters, Redheads, Ides, and then the Dupreys. But it finally became a private dwelling, the center of the surrounding farm, and no longer a public house.

Very little is known about its early history beyond what I've told here at least that is what Mrs. Florence Viner discovered when she considered buying the house. She did learn, however, that Mrs. Emery Duprey, a previous owner, had suffered great tragedy in the house. One morning she had taken a group of neighbor children to school. The school was in a one-room house, less than a mile distant. Her fourteen-year-old daughter Laura was left behind at the house because she had not been feeling well that day. When Mrs. Duprey returned home a short time later, she found the girl gone. Despite every effort made, the girl was never seen again nor was any trace found of her disappearance.

Mr. and Mrs. Charles Viner decided to buy the house in 1951 despite its deplorable condition. They wanted a large country house and did not mind putting it in good condition; in fact, they rather looked forward to the challenging task.

It was on Good Friday of that year that they moved in. Although they started the restoration immediately, they stayed at the house and made do, like the pioneers they felt they had now become.

The farm itself was still a working farm, and they retained a number of farm workers from the surrounding area to work it for them. The only people staying at the house at all times were the Viners, their daughter Sandra, and the help.

Two months after their arrival, one evening Mrs. Viner and her daughter, then eleven years old, were alone in the house, sitting in the kitchen downstairs, reading.

"Who is upstairs?" the girl suddenly inquired.

Mrs. Viner had heard furtive footsteps also, but had decided to ignore them. Surely, the old house was settling or the weather was causing all sorts of strange noises.

But the footsteps became clearer. This was no house settling. This was someone walking around upstairs. For several minutes, they sat in the kitchen, listening as the steps walked all over the upper floor. Then Mrs. Viner rose resolutely, went to her bedroom on the same floor and returned with a .22 revolver she had in the drawer of her night table just in case prowlers showed up. The moment she re-entered the kitchen, she clearly heard two heavy thumps upstairs. It sounded as if a couple of heavy objects had fallen suddenly and hit the floor. Abruptly, the walking ceased as if the thumps were the end of a scene being re-enacted upstairs.

Too frightened to go up and look into what she *knew* to be an empty room, Mrs. Viner went to bed. When her husband returned a little later, however, they investigated upstairs together. There was nothing out of place nor indeed any sign that anyone had been up there.

But a few days later, the same phenomenon recurred. First, there were the footsteps of someone walking up and down upstairs, as if in great agitation. Then two heavy thumps and the sound of a falling object and abrupt silence. The whole thing was so exactly the same each time it almost became part of the house routine, and the Viners heard it so many times they no longer became panicky because of it.

When the house regained its former splendor, they began to have overnight guests. But whenever anyone stayed at the house, inevitably, the next morning they would complain about the constant walking about in the corridor upstairs. Mrs. Ida Benoit, Mrs. Viner's mother, came downstairs the morning after her first night in the house and assured her daughter, "I'll never sleep in *this* house again. Why, it's haunted. Someone kept walking through my bedroom."

Her daughter could only shrug and smile wanly. She knew very well what her mother meant. Naturally, the number of unhappy guests grew, but she never discussed the phenomena with anyone beforehand. After all, it was just possible that *nothing* would happen. But in ten years of occupancy, there wasn't a single instance where a person using a bedroom upstairs was not disturbed.

A year after they had moved in, Mrs. Viner decided to begin to renovate a large upstairs bedroom. It was one of those often used as a guest room. This was on a very warm day in September, and despite the great heat, Mrs. Viner liked her work and felt in good spirits. She was painting the window sash and singing to herself with nothing particular on her mind. She was quite alone upstairs at the time and for the moment the ghostly phenomena of the past were far from her thoughts.

Suddenly, she felt the room grow ice cold. The chill became so intense she began to shudder and pulled her arms around herself as if she were in mid-winter on an icy road. She stopped singing abruptly and at the same time she felt the strong presence of another person in the room with her.

"Someone's resenting very much what I'm doing," she heard herself think.

Such a strong wave of hatred came over her she could not continue. Terrified, she nevertheless knew she had to turn around and see who was in the room with her. It seemed to take her an eternity to muster sufficient strength to move a single muscle.

Suddenly, she felt a cold hand at her shoulder. Someone was standing behind her and evidently trying to get her attention. She literally froze with fear. When she finally moved to see who it was the hand just melted away.

With a final effort, she jerked herself around and stared back into the room. There was no one there. She ran to the door, screaming, "I don't know who you are or what you are, but you won't drive me out of this house."

Still screaming, she ran down the stairs and onto the porch. There she caught her breath and quieted down. When her daughter came home from school, she felt relieved. The evil in that room had been overpowering, and she avoided going up there as much as possible after that experience.

"I'll never forget that hand, as long as I live," she explained to her husband.

In the years that followed, they came to terms with the unseen forces in the house. Perhaps her determined effort not to be driven out of her home had somehow gotten through to the specter. At any rate, the Viners were staying and making the house as livable as they could. Mrs. Viner gave birth to two more children, both sons, and as Sandra grew up, the phenomena seemed to subside. In 1958, a second daughter was born, and Sandra left for college. But three weeks later the trouble started anew.

One night in September, she was sitting in the downstairs livingroom watching television with James Latham, their farm worker. The two boys and the baby had been in bed for hours. Suddenly, there was a terrific explosion in the general direction of the baby's room. She ran into the room and found it ice cold — cold as an icebox. From the baby's room another door leads out into the hall, which was usually closed for obvious reasons. But now it stood wide open, evidently thrust open with considerable force. The lock was badly bent from the impact and the radiator, which the door had hit in opening, was still reverberating from it. The baby was not harmed in any way, but Mrs. Viner wondered if perhaps the oil burner had blown up.

She went down into the basement to check but found everything normal. As she returned to the baby's room she suddenly had the distinct impression that the phenomenon was somehow connected with the presence of a *young girl*.

Ghosts of New England

She tried to reason this away since no young girl was present in the household, nor was there any indication that this tied in in any way with the tragic disappearance of Mrs. Duprey's girl, of which she, of course, knew about. Try as she might, she could not shake this feeling that a young girl was the focal point of the disturbances at the house.

One night her sister had joined her in the livingroom downstairs. Suddenly there was a loud crash overhead in what they knew was an empty bedroom. Mrs. Viner left her worried sister downstairs and went up alone. A table in the bedroom had been knocked over. No natural force short of a heavy earthquake could have caused this. The windows were closed, and there was no other way in which the table could topple over by itself. She was so sure that this could not have been caused by anything but human intruders, she called the state police.

The police came and searched the house from top to bottom but found no trace of any intruder.

Mrs. Viner then began to wonder about the goings-on. If these unseen forces had the power to overturn heavy tables, surely they might also harm people. The thought frightened her. She had until then considered living with a ghost or ghosts rather on the chic side; now it took on distinctly threatening overtones. She discussed it with her husband but they had put so much work and money into the house that the thought of leaving again just did not appeal to them.

It was inevitable that she should be alone in the house, except for the children, at various times. Her husband was away on business, and the farm help were out where they belonged. Often Mrs. Viner found herself walking through the rooms hoping against rational reasoning that she would come face to face with the intruder. Then she could address her or him — she was not sure how many there were — and say, "Look, this is my house now, we've bought it and rebuilt it, and we don't intend to leave it. Go away and don't hang around; it's no use." She often rehearsed her little speech for just such a confrontation. But the ghost never appeared when she was ready.

Meanwhile the footsteps followed by the heavy thumps kept recurring regularly, often as many as four times in a single week. It was usually around the same time of the evening, which led her to believe that it represented some sort of tragedy that was being re-enacted upstairs by the ghostly visitors. Or was she merely tuning in on a past tragedy and what she and the others were hearing was in fact only an echo of the distant past? She could not believe this, especially as she still remembered vividly the ice cold hand that grabbed her shoulder in the bedroom upstairs on that hot September day. And a memory would not cause a heavy door to swing open by itself with such violence that it burst the lock.

No, these were not memory impressions they were hearing. These were actual entities with minds of their own, somehow trapped between two states of being and condemned by their own violence to live forever in the place where their tragedy had first occurred. What a horrible fate, Mrs. Viner thought, and for a moment she felt great compassion for the unfortunate ones.

But then her own involvement reminded her that it was, after all, her house and her life that was being disrupted. She had a better right to be here than they had, even if they had been here before.

Defiantly, she continued to polish and refine the appointments in the house until it looked almost as if it had never been a dilapidated, almost hopelessly derelict, house. She decided to repaper one of the bedrooms upstairs, so that her guests would sleep in somewhat more cheerful surroundings. The paper in this particular room was faded and very old and deserved to be replaced. As she removed the dirty wallpaper, the boards underneath became visible again. They were wide and smooth and obviously part of the original boards of the house.

After she had pulled down all the paper from the wall facing away from the window, she glanced up at it. The wall, exposed to light after goodness knows how many years, was spattered with some sort of paint.

"This won't do at all," she decided, and went downstairs to fetch some rags and water. Returning to the room, she started to remove what she took for some very old paint. When she put water on the stains, the spots turned a bright red!

Try as she might, she could not remove the red stains. Finally she applied some bleach, but it only turned the spots a dark brown. It finally dawned on her that this wasn't paint but blood. On closer investigation, her suspicion was confirmed. She had stumbled upon a blood-spattered wall — but what had taken place up here that had caused this horrible reminder?

Somehow she felt that she had gotten a lead in her quest for the solution to the phenomena plaguing the house. Surely, someone had been killed up there, but who and why?

She went into the village and started to talk to the local people. At first, she did not get much help. New Englanders are notoriously shy about family matters. But eventually Mrs. Viner managed to get some information from some of the older, local people who had known about the house on Brickyard Road for a long time.

When the house was still a public tavern, that is somewhere around the turn of the nineteenth century or the very end of the eighteenth, there had been two men at the tavern who stayed overnight as guests. Their names are shrouded in mystery, and perhaps they were very unimportant as history goes.

But there was also a young girl at the tavern, the kind innkeepers used to hire as servant girls in those days. If the girl wanted to be just that, well and good; if she wanted to get involved with some of the men that passed through on their way to the cities, that was her own business. Tavern keepers in those days were not moral keepers and the hotel detective had not yet been conceived by a Puritan age. So the servant girls often went in and out of the guests' rooms, and nobody cared much.

It appears that one such young girl was particularly attractive to two men at the same time. There were arguments and jealousy. Finally the two men retired to a room upstairs and a fight to the finish followed. As it was upstairs, most likely it was in the girl's own room, with one suitor discovering the other obtaining favors he had sought in vain, perhaps. At any rate, as the horrified girl looked on, the two men killed each other with their rapiers, and their blood, intermingled in death, spattered upon the wall of the room.

As she walked back from the village with this newly gained knowledge, Mrs. Viner understood clearly for the first time, why her house was indeed haunted. The restless footsteps in the room upstairs were the hurried steps of the unhappy suitor. The scuffling noises that followed and the sudden heavy thumps would be the fight and the two falling bodies — perhaps locked in death. The total silence that always ensued after the two heavy falls clearly indicated to her that the stillness of death following the struggle was being re-enacted along with the tragedy itself.

And how right she had been about a girl being the central force in all this!

But why the hostility towards her? Why the icy hand on the shoulder? Did the girl resent her, another woman, in this house? Was she still hoping her suitor would come for her, and did she perhaps take Mrs. Viner for competition? A demented mind, especially when it has been out of the body for a hundred and fifty years, can conjure up some strange ideas.

But her fighting energies were somehow spent, and when an opportunity arose to sell the house, Mrs. Viner agreed readily to do so. The house then passed into the hands of Samuel Beno after the

Viners had lived in it from 1951 to 1961. For five years, Mr. Beno owned the house but never lived in it. It remained unoccupied, standing quietly on the road.

Only once was there a flurry of excitement about it in recent years. In 1966 someone made off with $5,000 worth of plumbing and copper piping. The owner naturally entrusted the matter to the state police, hoping the thieves would eventually return for more. The authorities even placed tape recorders in the house in case the thieves did return.

Since then not much has been heard about the house and one can only presume that the tragic story of the servant girl and her two suitors has had its final run. But one can't be entirely sure until the next tenant moves into the old Lyons Tavern. After all, blood does not come off easily, either from walls or from men's memories.

The Old Merchant's House Ghost

Whuhen New York was still young and growing, a neighborhood that is now given over to derelicts and slums was an elegant, quiet area of homes and gardens. The world was right and peaceful in the young republic circa 1820. Gradually, however, the in people, as we call them nowadays, moved farther uptown, for such is the nature of a city confined to a small island. It can only move up, never down or out. Greenwich Village was still pretty far uptown, although the city had already spread beyond its limits, and the center of New York was somewhere around the city hall district (now considered way downtown).

Real estate developers envisioned the east side of Fifth Avenue as the place to put up elegant homes for the well-to-do. One of the more fashionable architects of that time was John McComb, who had plans for a kind of terrace of houses extending from Lafayette Street to the Bowery, with the back windows of the houses looking out on John Jacob Astor's property nearby. Now Mr. Astor was considered somewhat uncouth socially by some of his contemporaries (on one occasion he mistook a lady's voluminous sleeve for a dinner napkin), but nobody had any second thoughts about his prosperity or position in the commercial world. Thus, any house looking out upon such a desirable neighborhood would naturally attract a buyer, the builders reasoned, and they proved to be right.

Called brownstones because of the dark brick material of their facades, the houses were well-appointed and solid. Only one of them is still left in that area, while garages, factories, and ugly modern structures have replaced all the others.

The house in question was completed in 1830 and attracted the eagle eye of a merchant named Seabury Tredwell, who was looking for a proper home commensurate with his increasing financial status in the city. He bought it and moved in with his family.

Mr. Tredwell's business was hardware, and he was one of the proud partners in Kissam & Tredwell, with offices on nearby Dey Street. A portly man of fifty, Mr. Tredwell was what we would today call a conservative. One of his direct ancestors had been the first Episcopal bishop of New York, and though a merchant, Tredwell evinced all the outward signs of an emerging mercantile aristocracy. The house he acquired certainly looked the part: seven levels, consisting of three stories, an attic and two cellars, large, Federal style windows facing Fourth Street, a lovely garden around the house, and an imposing columned entrance door that one reached after ascending a flight of six marble stairs flanked by wrought-iron gate lanterns — altogether the nearest a merchant prince could come to a real nobleman in his choice of domicile.

Inside, too, the appointments are lavish and in keeping with the traditions of the times: a Duncan Phyfe banister ensconces a fine staircase leading to the three upper stories and originates in an elegant hall worthy of any caller.

As one steps into this hall, one first notices a huge, high-ceilinged parlor to the left. At the end of this parlor are mahogany double doors separating the room from the dining room, equally as large and impressive as the front room. The Duncan Phyfe table was at one time set with Haviland china and Waterford crystal, underlining the Tredwell family's European heritage. Each room has a large fireplace and long mirrors adding to the cavernous appearance of the two rooms. Large, floor-to-ceiling windows on each end shed light into the rooms, and when the mahogany doors are opened, the entire area looks like a ballroom in one of those manor houses Mr. Tredwell's forebears lived in in Europe.

The furniture — all of which is still in the house — was carefully chosen. Prominent in a corner of the parlor is a large, rectangular piano. Without a piano, no Victorian drawing room was worth its salt. A music box is on top for the delight of those unable to tinkle the ivories yet desirous of musical charms. The box plays "Home Sweet Home," and a sweet home it is indeed.

Farther back along the corridor one comes upon a small family room and a dark, ugly kitchen, almost L-shaped and utterly without charm or practical arrangements, as these things are nowadays understood. But in Victorian New York, this was a proper place to cook. Maidservants and cooks were not to be made cheerful, after all; theirs was to cook and serve, and not to enjoy.

On the first floor — or second floor, if you prefer, in today's usage — two large bedrooms are separated from each other by a kind of storage area, or perhaps a dressing room, full of drawers and cabinets. Off the front bedroom there is a small bedroom in which a four-poster bed takes up almost all the available space. The bed came over from England with one of Mrs. Tredwell's ancestors.

Leading to the third floor, the stairs narrow, and one is well advised to hold on to the banister lest he fall and break his neck. The third floor now serves as the curator's apartment. The Old Merchant's House is kept up as a private museum and is no longer at the mercy of the greedy wrecker. But when Seabury Tredwell lived in the house, the servants' rooms were on the third floor. Beyond that, a low-ceilinged attic provided additional space, and still another apartment fills part of the basement, also suitable for servants' usage.

All in all, it is the kind of house that inspires confidence in its owner. Mr. Tredwell's acquisition of the house helped establish him in New York society as a force to be reckoned with, for that, too, was good for his expanding business. He was eminently aided in this quest by the fact that his wife Eliza, whom he had married while still on his way up, had given him six daughters. Three of the girls made good marriages, left the parental homestead, and apparently made out very well, for not much was heard about them one way or another. Of the remaining three girls, however, plenty is recorded, and lots more is not, though it's undoubtedly true.

The three bachelor girls were named Phoebe, Sarah, and Gertrude. Phoebe's main interest was the Carl Fischer piano in the parlor, and she and her sister Sarah would often play together. Gertrude, the last of the Tredwell children, born in 1840, was different from the rest of them and kept herself apart. There were also two boys, but somehow they did not amount to very much, it is said, for it became necessary later, when of all the children only they and Gertrude were left, to appoint a cousin, Judge Seabury, to supervise the management of the estate. Brother Horace, in particular, was much more interested in tending the four magnolia trees that dominated the view from the tearoom.

To this day, nobody knows the real reason for a secret passage from a trap door near the bedrooms to the East River, a considerable distance. Recently, it was walled up to prevent rats from coming through it, but it is still there, holding on to its strange mystery — that is, to those who do not *know*.

Some of the things that transpired behind the thick walls of the Old Merchant's House would never have been brought to light were it not for the sensitive who walked its corridors a century later and piece for piece helped reconstruct what went on when the house was young. Only then did the various pieces of the jigsaw puzzle slowly sink into place, pieces that otherwise might never have found a common denominator.

When the house finally gave up its murky secrets, a strange calm settled over it, as if the story had wanted to be told after all those years to free it from the need of further hiding from the light.

* * *

Seabury Tredwell's stern Victorian ways did not sit well with all members of his family. The spinster girls in particular were both afraid of and respectful toward their father, and found it difficult to live up to his rigid standards. They wanted to marry but since no suitable person came along they were just as happy to wait. Underneath this resignation, however, a rebellious spirit boiled up in Sarah. Five years older than Gertrude, she could not or would not wait to find happiness in an age where the word scarcely had any personal meaning.

Tredwell ruled the family with an iron hand, demanding and getting blind submission to his orders. Thus it was with considerable misgivings that Sarah encouraged a budding friendship with a young man her father did not know, or know of, whom she had met accidentally at a tearoom. That in itself would have been sufficient reason for her father to disallow such a friendship. He was a man who considered anyone who referred to chicken *limbs* as legs, indecent. He ordered the legs of his chairs and tables covered, so they might not incite male visitors to unsavory ideas!

It took a great deal of ingenuity for Sarah to have a liaison with a strange man and not get caught. But her mother, perhaps out of rebellion against Tredwell, perhaps out of compassion for her neglected daughter, looked the other way, if not encouraged the relationship. And ingenious Sarah also found another ally in her quest for love. There was a Negro servant who had known and cared for her since her birth, and he acted as a go-between for her and the young man. For a few weeks, Sarah managed to sneak down to meet her paramour. Accidentally, she had discovered the secret passageway to the river and used it well. At the other end it led to what was then pretty rough ground and an even rougher neighborhood, but the young man was always there waiting with a carriage, and she felt far safer with him than in the cold embrace of her father's fanatical stare. Although Tredwell boasted to his friends that his house had "seven hundred locks and seven hundred keys," this was one door he had forgotten about.

Why an architect in 1830 would want to include a secret passageway is a mystery on the surface of it. But there were still riots in New York in those years, and the British invasion of 1812 was perhaps still fresh in some people's memories. A secret escape route was no more a luxury in a patrician American home than a priest hole was in a Catholic house in England. One never knew how things might turn. There had been many instances of slave rebellions, and the underground railroad, bringing the escapees up from the South, was in full swing then in New York.

One meeting with the young man, who shall remain nameless here, led to another, and before long, nature took its course. Sarah was definitely pregnant. Could she tell her father? Certainly not. Should they run off and marry? That seemed the logical thing to do, but Sarah feared the long arm of her family. Judge Seabury, her father's distinguished cousin, might very well stop them. Then too, there was the question of scandal. To bring scandal upon her family was no way to start a happy marriage.

Distraught, Sarah stopped seeing the young man. Nights she would walk the hallways of the house, sleepless from worry, fearful of discovery. Finally, she had to tell someone, and that someone was her sister Gertrude. Surprisingly, Gertrude did understand and comforted her as best she could. Now that they shared her secret, things were a little easier to bear. But unfortunately, things did not improve. It was not long before her father discovered her condition and all hell broke loose.

With the terror of the heavy he was, Tredwell got the story out of his daughter, except for the young man's name. This was especially hard to keep back, but Sarah felt that betraying her lover would not lead to a union with him. Quite rightfully, she felt her father would have him killed or jailed. When the old merchant discovered that there had been a go-between, and what was more, a man in his employ, the old Negro man was hauled over the coals. Only the fact that he had been with them for so many years and that his work was useful to the family prevented Tredwell from firing him immediately. But he abused the poor man and threatened him until the sheer shock of his master's anger changed his character: where he had been a pleasant and helpful servant, there was now only a shiftless, nervous individual, eager to avoid the light and all questions.

This went on for some weeks or months. Then the time came for the baby to be born and the master of the house had another stroke of genius. He summoned the black servant and talked with him at length. Nobody could hear what was said behind the heavy doors, but when the servant emerged his face was grim and his eyes glassy. Nevertheless, the old relationship between master and servant seemed to have been restored, for Tredwell no longer abused the man after this meeting.

What happened then we know only from the pieces of memory resurrected by the keen insight of a psychic: no court of law would ever uphold the facts as true in the sense the law requires, unfortunately, even if they are, in fact, true. One night there was a whimpering heard from the trapdoor between the two bedrooms upstairs, where there is now a chest of drawers and the walled-off passageway down to the river. Before the other servants in the house could investigate the strange noises in the night, it was all over and the house was silent again. Tredwell himself came from his room and calmed them.

"It is nothing," he said in stentorian tones, "just the wind in the chimney."

Nobody questioned the words of the master, so the house soon fell silent again.

But below stairs, in the dank, dark corridor leading to the river, a dark man carried the limp body of a newborn baby that had just taken its first, and last, breath.

Several days later, there was another confrontation. The evil doer wanted his pay. He had been promised a certain sum for the unspeakable deed. The master shrugged. The man threatened. The master turned his back. Who would believe a former slave, a runaway slave wanted down South? Truly, he didn't have to pay such a person. Evil has its own reward, too, and the dark man went back to his little room. But the imprint of the crime stuck to the small passage near the trap door and was picked up a century later by a psychic. Nobody saw the crime. Nobody may rightfully claim the arrangement between master and servant ever took place. But the house knows and its silence speaks louder than mere facts that will stand up in court.

When Sarah awoke from a stupor, days later, and found her infant gone, she went stark raving mad. For a time, she had to be restrained. Somehow, word leaked out into the streets of the city below, but no one ever dared say anything publicly. Sarah was simply indisposed to her friends. Weeks went by and her pain subsided. Gradually a certain relief filled the void inside her. She had lost everything, but at least her lover was safe from her father's clutches. Although she never knew for sure, whenever she glanced at the colored manservant, she shrank back: his eyes avoided her and her heart froze. Somehow, with the illogical knowledge of a mother, she *knew*. Then too, she avoided the passage near the trap door. Nothing could get her to walk through it. But as her health returned, her determination to leave also received new impetus. She could not go on living in this house where so much had happened. One day, she managed to get out of the door. It was a windy fall night, and she was badly dressed for it. Half-mad with fear of being followed, she roamed the streets for hours. Darkness and her mental condition took their toll. Eventually she found herself by the water. When she was found, she was still alive, but expired before she could be brought back to the house.

Her death — by her own hands — was a blow to the family. Word was given out that Sarah had died in a carriage accident. It sounded much more elegant, and though no one ever found out what carriage, as she had been in bed for so long, and just learned to walk about the house again, it was accepted because of the unspoken code among the Victorians: one man's tragedy is never another's gossip. Then, too, the question of suicide was a thorny one to resolve in an age that had not yet freed the human personality even in the flesh: it had to be an accident.

Thus Sarah was laid to rest along with the others of her family in the Christ Churchyard in Manhasset, Long Island, properly sanctified as behooves the daughter of an important citizen whose ancestor was a bishop.

What had happened to Sarah did not pass without making a deep and lasting impression on the youngest girl, Gertrude, who was called Gitty when she was young. She tried not to talk about it, of course, but it made her more serious and less frivolous in her daily contacts.

She was now of the age where love can so easily come, yet no one had held her hand with the slightest effect on her blood pressure. True, her father had introduced a number of carefully screened young men, and some not so young ones, in the hope that she might choose one from among them. But Gertrude would not marry just to please her father, yet she would not marry against his wishes. There had to be someone she could love and whom her father could also accept, she reasoned, and she was willing to wait for him.

While she was playing a game with time, spring came around again, and the air beckoned her to come out into the garden for a walk. While there, she managed to catch the eye of a young man on his way past the house. Words were exchanged despite Victorian propriety, and she felt gay and giddy.

She decided she would not make the mistake her sister had made in secretly seeing a young man. Instead, she encouraged the shy young man, whose name was Louis, to seek entry into her house openly and with her father's knowledge, if not yet blessings. This he did, not without difficulties, and Seabury Tredwell had him investigated immediately. He learned that the young man was a penniless student of medicine.

"But he'll make a fine doctor someday," Gertrude pleaded with her father.

"Someday," the old man snorted. "And what is he going to live on until then? I tell you what. *My* money."

Tredwell assumed, and perhaps not without reason, that everybody in New York knew that his daughters were heiresses and would have considerable dowries as well. This idea so established itself in his mind, he suspected every gentleman caller of being a fortune hunter. The young man was, of course, he argued, not after his daughter's love, but merely her money and that would never do.

Gertrude was no raving beauty although she possessed a certain charm and independence. She was petite, with a tiny waistline, blue eyes and dark hair, and she greatly resembled Britain's Princess Margaret when the latter was in her late twenties.

Tredwell refused to accept the young medical student as a

serious suitor. Not only was the young man financially unacceptable, but worse, he was a Catholic. Tredwell did not believe in encouraging marriages out of the faith and even if Louis had offered to change religions, it is doubtful the father would have changed his mind. In all this he paid absolutely no heed to his daughter's feelings or desires, and with true Victorian rigidity, forbade her to see the young man further.

There was finally a showdown between father and daughter. Tredwell, no longer so young, and afflicted with the pains and aches of advancing age, pleaded with her not to disappoint him in his last remaining years. He wanted a good provider for her, and Louis was not the right man. Despite her feelings, Gertrude finally succumbed to her father's pleading and sent the young man away. When the doors closed on him for the last time, it was as if the gates of Gertrude's heart had also permanently closed on the outside world: hence she lived only for her father and his well-being and no young man ever got to see her again.

Seabury Tredwell proved a difficult and thankless patient as progressive illness forced him to bed permanently. When he finally passed away in 1865, the two remaining sisters, Gertrude and Phoebe, continued to live in the house. But it was Gertrude who ran it. They only went out after dark and only when absolutely necessary to buy food. The windows were always shuttered and even small leaks covered with felt or other material to keep out the light and cold.

As the two sisters cut themselves off from the outside world, all kinds of legends sprang up about them. But after Phoebe died and left Gertrude all alone in the big house, even the legends stopped and gradually the house and its owner sank into the oblivion afforded yesterday's sensation by a relentless, everchanging humanity.

Finally, at age ninety-three, Gertrude passed on. The year was 1933, and America had bigger headaches than what to do about New

York's last authentic brownstone. The two servants who had shared the house with Gertrude to her death, and who had found her peacefully asleep, soon left, leaving the house to either wreckers or new owners, or just neglect. There was neither electricity nor telephone in it, but the original furniture and all the fine works of art Seabury Tredwell had put into the house were still there. The only heat came from fireplaces with which the house was filled. The garden had long gone, and only the house remained, wedged in between a garage and nondescript modern building. Whatever elegance there had been was now present only inside the house or perhaps in the aura of its former glories.

The neighborhood was no longer safe, and the house itself was in urgent need of repairs. Eventually, responsible city officials realized the place should be made into a museum, for it presented one of the few houses in America with everything — from furniture to personal belongings and clothes — still intact as it was when people lived in it in the middle of the nineteenth century. There were legal problems of clearing title, but eventually this was done and the Old Merchant's House became a museum.

*   *   *

When the first caretaker arrived to live in the house, it was discovered that thieves had already broken in and made off with a pair of Sheffield candelabra, a first edition of Charlotte Bronte, and the Tredwell family Bible. But the remainder was still intact, and a lot of cleaning up had to be done immediately.

One of the women helping in this work found herself alone in the house one afternoon. She had been busy carrying some of Miss Gertrude's clothing downstairs so that it could be properly displayed in special glass cases. When she rested from her work for a moment, she looked up and saw herself being watched intently by a woman on the stairs. At first glance, she looked just like Princess Margaret of England, but then she noticed the strange old-fashioned clothes the woman wore and realized she belonged to another age. The tight fitting bodice had a row of small buttons and the long, straight skirt reached to the floor. As the volunteer stared in amazement at the stranger, wondering who it could be, the girl on the stairs vanished.

At first the lady did not want to talk about her experience, but when it happened several times, and always when she was alone in the house, she began to wonder whether she wasn't taking leave of her senses. But soon another volunteer moved into the picture, a lady writer who had passed the house on her way to the library to do some research. Intrigued by the stately appearance of the house, she looked into it further and before long was in love with the house.

There was a certain restlessness that permeated the building after dark, but she blamed it on her imagination and the strange neighborhood. She did not believe in ghosts nor was she given to fancies, and the noises didn't really disturb her.

She decided that there was a lot of work to be done if the museum were to take its proper place among other showplaces, and she decided to give the tourists and other visitors a good run for their money — all fifty cents' worth of it.

The next few weeks were spent in trying to make sense out of the masses of personal effects, dresses, gowns, shoes, hats. The Tredwells had left everything behind them intact — as if they had intended to return to their earthly possessions one of these days and to resume life as it was.

Nothing had been given away or destroyed and Mrs. R., writer that she was, immediately realized how important it was that the residence be kept intact for future research of that period. She went to work at once and as she applied herself to the job at hand, she began to get the *feel* of the house as if she had herself lived in it for many years.

She started her job by taking an inventory of the late Gertrude Tredwell's wardrobe once again. This time the job had to be done properly, for the visitors to the museum were entitled to see a good display of period costumes. As she picked through Gertrude's vast wardrobe one article at a time, she had the uncanny feeling of being followed step for step. The house was surrounded by slums and the danger of real break-ins very great, but this was different: no flesh and blood intruders followed her around on her rounds from the third floor down to the basement and back again for more clothes.

Often a chilly feeling touched her as she walked through the halls, but she attributed that to the moist atmosphere in the old house.

One day when she entered the front bedroom that used to be Gertrude's, from the hall bedroom, she had the distinct impression of another presence close to her. Something was brushing by her to reach the other door that opened into the front bedroom before she did!

When this happened again sometime later, she began to wonder if the stories about the house being haunted, which circulated freely in the neighborhood, did not have some basis in fact. Certainly there was a presence, and the sound of another person brushing past her was quite unmistakable.

While she was still deliberating whether or not to discuss this with any of her friends, an event took place that brought home the suspicion that she was never quite alone in the house.

It was on a morning several months after her arrival, that she walked into the kitchen carrying some things to be put into the display cases ranged along the wall opposite the fireplace. Out of the corner of her eye she caught sight of what looked like the figure of a small, elegant woman standing in front of this huge fireplace. While Mrs. R. was able to observe the brown taffeta gown she was wearing, her head was turned away, so she could not see her features. But there were masses of brown hair. The whole thing was in very soft focus, rather misty without being insubstantial. Her hands, however, holding a cup and saucer, were very beautiful and quite sharply defined against her dark gown.

Mrs. R. was paralyzed, afraid to turn her head to look directly at her. Suddenly, however, without any conscious volition, she spun around and quickly walked out of the room into the hall. By the time she got to the stairs she was covered with cold perspiration, and her hands were shaking so violently she had to put down the things she was carrying.

Now she knew that Gertrude Tredwell was still around, but not the way she looked when she died. Rather, she had turned back her memory clock to that period of her life when she was gayest and her young man had not yet been sent away by a cruel and unyielding father.

When the realization came to Mrs. R. as to who her ghostly friend was, her fears went away. After all, who would have a better right to be in this house than the one who had sacrificed her love and youth to it and what it stood for in her father's view. This change of her attitude must have somehow gotten through to the ghostly lady as well, by some as yet undefinable telegraph connecting all things, living and dead.

Sometime thereafter, Mrs. R. was arranging flowers for the table in the front parlor. The door was open to the hallway and she was quite alone in the house. She was so preoccupied with the flower arrangement, she failed to notice that she was no longer alone.

Finally, a strange sound caught her attention, and she looked up from the table. The sound was that of a taffeta gown swishing by in rapid movement. As her eyes followed the sound, she saw a woman going up the stairs. It was the same, petite figure she had originally seen at the fireplace sometime before. Again she wore the brown taffeta gown. As she rounded the stairs and disappeared from view, the sound of the gown persisted for a moment or two after the figure herself had gotten out of sight.

This time Mrs. R. did not experience any paralysis or fear. Instead, a warm feeling of friendship between her and the ghost sprang up within her, and contentedly, as if nothing had happened, she continued with her flower arrangement.

During this time, the curator of the Old Merchant's House was a professional antiquarian named Janet Hutchinson who shared the appointments with her friend Emeline Paige, editor of *The Villager*, a neighborhood newspaper, and Mrs. Hutchinson's son, Jefferson, aged fourteen. In addition, there was a cat named Eloise who turned out to be a real fraidicat for probably good and valid reasons.

Although Mrs. Hutchinson did not encounter anything ghostly during her tenure, the lady editor did feel very uneasy in the back bedroom, where much of the tragedy had taken place.

Another person who felt the oppressive atmosphere of the place, without being able to rationalize it away for any good reasons, was Elizabeth Byrd, the novelist, and her friend, whom I must call Mrs. B., for she shies away from the uncanny in public. Mrs. B. visited the house one evening in 1964. As she stood in what had once been Gertrude's bedroom, she noticed that the bedspread of Gertrude's bed was indented *as if someone had just gotten up from it*. Clearly, the rough outline of a body could be made out.

As she stared in disbelief at the bed, she noticed a strange perfume, in the air. Those with her remarked on the scent, but before anyone could look for its sources, it had evaporated. None of the ladies with Mrs. B. had on any such perfume, and the house had been sterile and quiet for days.

Since that time, no further reports of any unusual experiences have come to mind. On one occasion in 1965, photographs of the fireplace near which Mrs. R. had seen the ghost of Gertrude Tredwell were taken simultaneously by two noted photographers with equipment previously tested for proper functioning. This was done to look into the popular legend that this fireplace could not be photographed and that whenever anyone attempted it, that person would have blank film as a result. Perhaps the legend was started by a bad photographer, or it was just that, a legend, for both gentlemen produced almost identical images of the renowned fireplace with their cameras. However, Gertrude Tredwell was not standing in front of it.

This is as it should be. Mrs. R., the untiring spirit behind the Historical Landmarks Society that keeps the building going and out of the wreckers' hands, feels certain that Gertrude need not make another appearance now that everything is secure. And to a Victorian lady, that matters a great deal.

The Old Merchant's House, forever threatened by the wrecker's ball, receives visitors Sundays from 1 to 4. I saw it last about a year ago, as I write these lines in 1988, with a psychic lady named Kathleen Roach. Directly she stepped inside Gertrude's parlor, she turned around and asked me to get her out of the house; the jealousy and anger of the old girl evidently never left the house. So if you happen to run into her, be kind.

The Ghosts at the Morris-Jumel Mansion

We had hardly returned to our home in New York, when my friend Elizabeth Byrd telephoned to inquire if I had gotten that grave opened yet. I hadn't, but I should really let you in at the beginning.

You see, it all started with an article in the *New York Journal-American* on January 11, 1964, by Joan Hanauer, in which the ghostly goings-on at Jumel Mansion in New York City were brought to public attention. Youngsters on a field trip from P.S. 164, Edgecombe Avenue and 164th Street, said a tall, gray-haired, elderly woman stepped out onto the balcony and told them to be quiet.

The description fit Mme. Jumel.

Could it have happened?

Mrs. Emma Bingay Campbell, curator of the Mansion at 160th Street and Edgecombe, said no.

"I don't believe in ghosts," she said, "but it was very strange. The house was locked and empty. We know that. There could not have been a woman there. But several of the children insist they saw and heard her.

"It was shortly before 11, opening time for the house, which dates back to 1765.

"When I came over to the children to explain they must wait for John Duffy, the second gardener, to unlock the doors at 11," Mrs. Campbell said, "one of the girls wanted to know why the tall woman who had come out on the balcony to reprimand them for boisterousness couldn't let them in. There couldn't have been any such woman — or anyone else — in the house.

"The woman the children described resembled Mme. Jumel, who some thought murdered her husband in the house in 1832, then married Aaron Burr the following year.

"But the children couldn't know that, or what she looked like.

"They also couldn't know that the balcony on which the apparition appeared separated Mme. Jumel's and Burr's bedrooms."

Elizabeth Byrd was then working on a story about Manhattan ghosts for a magazine, so we decided to follow up this case together. First we contacted the public school authorities and obtained permission to talk to the children. The teacher assembled the entire group she had originally taken to the Jumel Mansion, and we questioned them, separately and together. Their story was unchanged. The woman appeared on the balcony, suddenly, and she told them to be quiet.

"How did she disappear?" I wanted to know.

One youngster thought for a moment, then said hesitantly, "She sort of glided back into the house."

"Did you see the balcony doors open?" I asked the girl.

"No, sir," she replied firmly.

"Then did she glide through the door?"

"She did."

The dress they described the ghost as wearing does exist — but it is put away carefully upstairs in the mansion and was not on display, nor is this common knowledge, especially among eleven-year-old schoolgirls.

There was a cooking class in progress when we arrived, and the girls cheerfully offered us samples of their art. We declined for the moment and went on to see the curator of the mansion, Mrs. Campbell. This energetic lady takes care of the mansion for the Daughters of the American Revolution in whose charge the City of New York had placed the museum.

"Is this the first report of a haunting here?" I wanted to know.

Mrs. Campbell shook her head. "Here," she said, and took down from one of the shelves in her office a heavy book. "William Henry Shelton's work, *The Jumel Mansion*, pages two hundred and seven and two hundred and eight report earlier ghosts observed here."

"Have you ever seen or heard anything?"

"No, not yet, but others have. There was that German nurse who lived here in eighteen sixty-five — she heard strange noises even then. Footsteps have been heard by many visitors here when there was no one about. The ghost of Mme. Jumel appeared to a retired guard at the door of this room."

"How would you like me to investigate the matter?" I offered. A date was set immediately.

First, I thought it wise to familiarize myself with the physical layout of the historic house. I was immediately struck by its imposing appearance. Historian John Kent Tilton wrote:

> Located on the highest elevation of Manhattan is one of the most famous old historic houses in the nation, the Morris-Jumel Mansion. The locality was originally called Harlem Heights by the Dutch in the days of New Amsterdam and was then changed to Mount Morris during the English ownership, before receiving the present name of Washington Heights.

The plot of land upon which the old mansion is situated was originally deeded in 1700 to a Dutch farmer named Jan Kiersen, from part of the "half morgen of land of the common woods" of New Haarlem.

Lieutenant Colonel Roger Morris purchased the estate in 1765. The new owner was born in England in 1728 and came to America at the age of eighteen with a commission of captaincy in the British army.

It was here that the Morris family, with their four children, spent their summers, living the domestic life typical of a British squire and family until the outbreak of the Revolution.

Colonel Morris fled to England at the beginning of hostilities, where he remained for two and one-half years.

As early in the war as August 1776, Mount Morris was taken over by the American troops and General Heath and staff were quartered there. After the disastrous Battle of Long Island, General Washington retreated to Haarlem Heights and made the place his headquarters. After Washington decided to abandon this location, the British moved in and the Morris Mansion housed General Sir Henry Clinton and his officers and, at intervals, the Hessians, during the seven years the British occupied New York.

During the following quarter of a century it was sold and resold several times and witnessed many changes in its varied career. Renamed Calumet Hall, it served for a time as a Tavern and was a stopping place for the stage coaches en route to Albany. It was the home of an unknown farmer when President Washington paid a visit to his old headquarters and entertained at dinner, among others, his cabinet members, John Adams, Alexander Hamilton, Henry Knox, and their wives.

The locality was one that Stephen Jumel with his sprightly and ambitious wife delighted driving out to on a summer's day from their home on Whitehall Street. Mme. Jumel became entranced with the nearby old Morris Mansion and persuaded her husband to purchase it for their home in 1810, for the sum of $10,000 which included 35 acres of land still remaining of the original tract.

The old house was fast falling into decay when Mme. Jumel energetically went about renovating and refurnishing it, and when completed, it was one of the most beautiful homes in the country. The Jumels restored the mansion in the style of the early nineteenth century, when the Federal influence was in fashion.

Mme. Jumel first married, some say by trickery, the rich Frenchman, Stephen Jumel. He had at one time owned a large plantation in Santo Domingo from whence he was obliged to flee at the time of the insurrection. Arriving in the United States, a comparatively poor man, he soon amassed a new fortune as a wine merchant, and at his death in 1832, his wife became one of the richest women in America. A year later she married Aaron Burr, former vice president of the United States. This second marriage, however, was of short duration and ended in divorce. Mme. Jumel died at the age of 93 in 1865.

The Morris-Jumel Mansion is of the mid-Georgian period of architecture. The front facade has four columns, two stories in height, with a pediment at the top.

The exterior is painted white. One of the post-Colonial features added by the Jumels is the imposing front entrance doorway, with flanking sidelights and elliptical fanlight.

In the interior, the wide central hall with arches is furnished with late eighteenth and early nineteenth century pieces. At the left of the entrance is the small parlor or tearoom where the marriage ceremony of the Widow Jumel and Aaron Burr was performed in 1833 when the bride was fifty-eight and the groom twenty years her senior.

Across the hall is the stately Georgian dining room where many persons of fame assembled for elaborate dinner parties.

At the rear of the hall is the large octagonal drawing room.

The broad stairway leads to the spacious hall on the upper floor, which is furnished with personal belongings of the Jumels. There is a group portrait of Mme. Jumel and the young son and daughter of her adopted daughter, Mary Eliza, who married Nelson Chase.

The northwest bedroom contains furniture owned by the Jumels, including a carved four-poster bed.

In the old days the rooms on the third floor were probably used as extra guest chambers since the servants' quarters were then located in the basement with the kitchen.

On January 19, 1964, a small group of people assembled in Betsy Jumel's old sitting room upstairs. Present were a few members of the New York Historical Society and the Daughters of the American Revolution, *Journal-American* writer Nat Adams, and a late-comer, Harry Altschuler of the *World-Telegram*. I was accompanied by Ethel Meyers, who had not been told where we were going that winter afternoon, and Jessyca Russell Gaver, who was serving as my secretary and doing a magazine article on our work at the same time.

We had barely arrived when Ethel went in and out of the Jumel bedroom as if someone were forcing her to do so. As she approached the room across the hall, her shoulder sagged and one arm hung loose as if her side had been injured!

"I feel funny on my left side," Ethel finally said, and her voice had already taken on some of the coloring of someone else's voice.

We went back to the bedroom, which is normally closed to the public. One side is occupied by a huge carved four-poster, once the property of Napoleon I, and there are small chairs of the period in various spots throughout the room. In one corner, there is a large mirror.

"The issue is confused," Ethel said, and sounded confused herself. "There is more than one disturbed person here. I almost feel as though three people were involved. There has been sickness and a change of heart. Someone got a raw deal."

Suddenly, Ethel turned to one of the men who had sat down on Napoleon's bed. "Someone wants you to get up from that bed," she said, and evinced difficulty in speaking. As if bitten by a tarantula, the young man shot up from the bed. No ghost was going to goose *him*.

Ethel again struggled to her feet, despite my restraining touch on her arm. "I've got to go back to that other room again," she mumbled, and off she went, with me trailing after her. She walked almost as if she were being taken over by an outside force. In front of the picture of Mme. Jumel, she suddenly fell to her knees.

"I never can go forward here . . . I fall whenever I'm near there." She pointed at the large picture above her, and almost shouted, "My name isn't on that picture. I want my name there!"

Mrs. Campbell, the curator, took me aside in agitation. "That's very strange she should say that," she remarked. "You see, her name really used to be on that picture a long time ago. But that picture wasn't in this spot when Betsy Jumel was alive."

I thanked her and led Ethel Meyers back to her chair in the other room.

"Henry . . . and a Johann . . . around her . . . ," she mumbled as she started to go into a deep trance. Hoarse sounds emanated from her lips. At first they were unintelligible. Gradually I was able to make them out. Halfway into a trance, she moved over to the bed and lay down on it. I placed my chair next to her head. The others strained to hear. There was an eerie silence about the room, interrupted only by the soft words of the entranced medium.

"You think me dead . . . " a harsh, male voice now said.

"No, I've come to talk to you, to help you," I replied.

"Go away," the ghostly voice said. "Go away!"

"Are you a man or a woman?" I asked.

A bitter laugh was the reply.

"Man . . . ha!" the voice finally said.

"What is your name?"

"Everybody knows who I am."

"I don't. What is your name?" I repeated.

"Let me sleep."

"Is anything troubling you?"

There was a moment of silence, then the voice was a bit softer. "Who are *you?*"

"I'm a friend come to help you."

"Nobody talks to me. They think I'm dead."

"What exactly happened to you?"

"They took me away," the voice said in plaintive tones. "I am not dead yet. Why did they take me away?"

Now the body of the medium shook as if in great agitation, while I spoke soothing words to calm the atmosphere. Suddenly, the ghost speaking through the medium was gone, and in his place was the crisp, matter-of-fact voice of Albert, Ethel's control. I asked Albert to tell us through the entranced medium who the ghost was.

"I don't hear a name, but I see a sturdy body and round face. He complains he was pronounced dead when he in fact wasn't. I believe he is the owner of the house and it bears his name. There are many jealousies in this house. There is an artist who is also under suspicion."

"Is there a woman here?"

"One thwarted of what she desired and who wants to throw herself out the window."

"Why?" I asked.

"Thwarted in love and under suspicion."

Later, I asked Mrs. Campbell about this. She thought for a moment, then confirmed the following facts: A young servant girl involved with one of the family tried to commit suicide by jumping out the window.

I questioned Albert further. "Is there a restless woman in this house?"

"That is right. The one in the picture. Her conscience disturbs her."

"About what?"

The medium now grabbed her side, as if in pain. "I am being threatened," Albert said now, "I feel the revelation would disturb."

"But how can I release her unless I know what is holding her here?"

"It has to do with the death of her husband. That he was strangled in his coffin."

I tried to question him further, but he cut us short. The medium had to be released now.

Soon, Ethel Meyers was back to her own self. She remembered very little of the trance, but her impressions of a clairvoyant nature continued for a while. I queried her about the person on the bed.

"I get the initial J," she replied and rubbed her side.

I turned to Mrs. Campbell. "What about the story of Mme. Jumel's guilty conscience?"

"Well," the curator replied, "after her husband's death, she refused to live in this house for some time. She always felt guilty about it."

We were standing in a corner where the medium could not hear us. "Stephen Jumel bled to death from a wound he had gotten in a carriage accident. Mme. Jumel allegedly tore off his bandage and let him die. That much we know."

Mrs. Campbell naturally is a specialist on Betsy Jumel and her life, and she knows many intimate details unknown to the general public or even to researchers.

It was five-thirty in the afternoon when we left the house, which must be closed for the night after that hour.

*　*　*

The next morning two newspaper accounts appeared: One, fairly accurate, in the *Journal,* and a silly one in the *Telegram,* by a man who stood outside the room of the investigation and heard very little, if anything.

Several weeks went by and my ghost-hunting activities took me all over the country. Then I received a telephone call from Mrs. Campbell.

"Did you know that May twenty-second is the anniversary of Stephen Jumel's death?" I didn't and I wagered her nobody else did, except herself and the late Mr. Jumel. She allowed as to that and suggested we have another go at the case on that date. I have always felt that anniversaries are good times to solve murder cases so I readily agreed.

This time, the *Journal* and *Telegram* reporters weren't invited, but the *New York Times,* in the person of reporter Grace Glueck, was, and I am indebted to her for the notes she took of the proceedings that warm May afternoon.

Present also were the general manager of King Features, Frank McLearn; Clark Kinnaird, literary critic of the *Journal;* John Allen and Bob O'Brien of *Reader's Digest;* Emeline Paige, the editor of *The Villager;* writers Elizabeth Byrd and Beverly Balin; Ed Joyce of CBS; and several members of the New York Historical Society, presumably there as observers ready to rewrite history as needed since the famous Aaron Burr might be involved.

Ethel Meyers was told nothing about the significance of the date, nor had I discussed with her the results of the first seance.

Again we assembled in the upstairs bedroom and Ed Joyce set up his tape recorder in front of Napoleon's bed, while Ethel sat on the bed itself and I next to her on a chair. To my left, the young lady from the *Times* took her seat. All in all there must have been twenty-five anxious people in the room, straining to hear all that was said and keeping a respectful silence when asked to. Within a few minutes, Ethel was in a deep trance, and a male voice spoke through her vocal chords.

"Who are you?" I asked as I usually do when an unknown person comes through a medium.

"*Je suis Stephen,*" the voice said.

"Do you speak English?"

In answer the medium clutched at her body and groaned, "Doctor! Doctor! Where is the doctor?"

"What is hurting you?" I asked.

The voice was firm and defiant now. "I'm alive, I'm alive . . . don't take me away."

"Did you have an accident? What happened to you?"

"She tricked me."

"Who tricked you?"

"I can't breathe . . . where is she? She tricked me. Look at her!"

"Don't worry about her," I said. "She's dead."

"But I'm alive!" the entranced voice continued.

"In a sense, you are. But you have also passed over."

"No — they put me in the grave when I was not yet dead."

"How did you get hurt?" I wanted to know.

The ghost gave a bitter snort. "What matter — I'm dead. You said so."

"I didn't say you were dead." I replied.

The voice became furious again. "She took it, she took it — that woman. She took my life. Go away."

"I'm your friend."

"I haven't any friends . . . that Aaron . . ."

"Aaron? Was he involved in your death?"

"That strumpet . . . hold him! They buried me alive, I tell you."

"When did this happen?"

"It was cold. She made me a fool, a fool!"

"How did she do that?"

"All the time I loved her, she tricked me."

"I want to help you."

"I'm bleeding."

"How did this happen?"

"Pitchfork . . . wagon . . . hay . . . "

"Was it an accident, yes or no?"

"I fell on it."

"You fell on the pitchfork?"

"Look at the blood bath . . . on Napoleon's bed."

"What about that pitchfork?" I insisted.

"There was a boy in the hay, and he pushed me off."

"Did you know this boy?"

"Yes . . . give me *her*. She wanted to be a lady. I saw it. I wasn't so foolish I didn't see it."

"What happened when you got home?"

"She told me I was going to die."

"Did you have a doctor?"

"Yes."

"Wasn't the wound bandaged?"

"They took me out alive. I was a live man he put in the grave. I want to be free from that grave!"

"Do you want me to set you free?"

"God bless you!"

"It is your hatred that keeps you here. You must forgive."

"She did it to me."

I then pleaded with the ghost to join his own family and let go of his memories. "Do you realize how much time has gone on since? A hundred years!"

"Hundred years!"

The medium, still entranced, buried her head in her hands: "I'm mad!"

"Go from this house and don't return."

"Mary, Mary!"

Mary was the name of Jumel's daughter, a fact not known to the medium at the time.

"Go and join Mary!" I commanded, and asked that Albert, the control, help the unhappy one find the way.

Just as soon as Jumel's ghost had left us, someone else slipped into the medium's body, or so it seemed, for she sat up and peered at us with a suspicious expression: "Who are you?"

"I'm a friend, come to help," I replied.

"I didn't ask for you."

"My name is Holzer, and I have come to seek you out. If you have a name worth mentioning, please tell us."

"Get out or I'll call the police! This is my house."

There was real anger now on the medium's entranced face.

I kept asking for identification. Finally, the disdainful lips opened and in cold tones, the voice said, "I am the wife of the vice president of the United States! Leave my house!"

I checked with Mrs. Campbell and found that Betsy Jumel did so identify herself frequently. On one occasion, driving through crowded New York streets long after her divorce from Aaron Burr, she shouted, "Make way for the wife of the vice president of the United States!"

"Didn't you marry someone else before that?" I asked. "How did your husband die?"

"Bastard!"

"You've been dead a hundred years, Madam," I said pleasantly.

"You are made like the billow in the captain's cabin," she replied, somewhat cryptically. Later I checked this out. A sea captain was one of her favorite lovers while married to Jumel.

"Did you murder your husband?" I inquired and drew back a little just in case.

"You belong in the scullery with my maids," she replied disdainfully, but I repeated the accusation, adding that her husband had claimed she had killed him.

"I will call for help," she countered.

"There is no help. The police are on your trail!" I suggested.

"I am the wife of the vice president of the United States!"

"I will help you if you tell me what you did. Did you cause his death?"

"The rats that crawl . . . they bit me. Where am I?"

"You're between two worlds. Do you wish to be helped?"

"Where is Joseph?"

"You must leave this house. Your husband has forgiven you."

"I adored him!"

"Go away, and you will see Stephen Jumel again."

"Only the crest on the carriage! That's all I did. He was a great man."

I had the feeling she wasn't at all keen on Monsieur Jumel. But that happens, even to ghosts.

I finally gave up trying to get her to go and join Jumel and tried another way.

"Go and join the vice president of the United States. He awaits you." To my surprise, this didn't work either.

"He is evil, evil," she said.

Perplexed, I asked, "Whom do you wish to join?"

"Mary."

"Then call out her name, and she'll join you and take you with her."

"No crime, no crime."

"You've been forgiven. Mary will take you away from here."

I asked Albert, the control, to come and help us get things moving, but evidently Madame had a change of heart: "This is my house. I'll stay here."

"This is no longer your house. You must go!"

The struggle continued. She called for Christopher, but wouldn't tell me who Christopher was.

"He's the only one I ever trusted," she volunteered, finally.

"It's not too late," I repeated. "You can join your loved ones."

"Good-bye."

I called for Albert, who quickly took control. "She's no longer in the right mind," he said, as soon as he had firm control of the medium's vocal chords. "You may have to talk with her again."

"Is she guilty of Jumel's death?"

"Yes. It was arranged."

"Who was the boy who pushed him?"

"A trusty in the house. She told him to."

"What about Stephen Jumel?"

"He is in a better frame of mind."

"Is there anything else we did not bring out? Who is this Christopher she mentioned?"

"A sea captain. She buried him in Providence."

Mrs. Campbell later confirmed the important role the sea captain played in Betsy's life. There was also another man named Brown.

"Did Aaron Burr help bury Jumel?"

"That is true. Burr believed Mme. Jumel had more finances than she actually had."

"What about the doctor who buried him alive? Is his name known?"

"Couldn't stop the bleeding."

"Was Aaron Burr in on the crime?"

"He is very much aware that he is guilty. He still possesses his full mental faculties."

I then asked the control to help keep the peace in the house and to bring the medium back to her own body.

A few minutes later, Ethel Meyers was herself again, remembering nothing of the ordeal she had gone through the past hour, and none the worse for it.

Jumel died in 1832 and, as far as I could find, the first ghostly reports date back to 1865. The question was: Could his remains disclose any clues as to the manner in which he died? If he suffocated in his coffin, would not the position of his bones so indicate?

I queried two physicians who disagreed in the matter. One thought that nothing would be left by now; the other thought it was worth looking into.

I thought so, too. However, my application to reopen the grave of Stephen Jumel, down in the old Catholic cemetery on Mott Street, got the official run-around. The District Attorney's office sent me to Dr. Halpern, the chief medical examiner, who told me it would be of no use to check. When I insisted, I was referred to the church offices of old St. Patrick's, which has nominal jurisdiction over the plot.

Have you ever tried to reopen a grave in the City of New York? It's easier to dig a new one, believe me!

As the years passed, I often returned to the mansion. I made several television documentaries there with the helpful support of the curator, who now is the affable and knowledgeable Patrick Broom. The famous blue gown is no longer on display, alas, having disintegrated shortly after I first published the story. But the legend persists, and the footfalls are still heard on lonely nights when the security guard locks up. Whether the Jumels, the remorseful Betsy and the victimized Stephen, have since made up on the Other Side, is a moot question, and I doubt that Aaron Burr will want anything further to do with the, ah, lady, either.

ALSO BY HANS HOLZER

Ghosts and Hauntings

Gothic Ghosts
Haunted Hollywood
Ghost Hunter
Ghosts I've Met
The Phantoms of Dixie
The Lively Ghosts of Ireland
Westghosts
The Ghosts That Walked in Washington
The Spirits of '76
Hans Holzer's Haunted Houses
The Ghost Hunter's Strangest Cases
Some of My Best Friends Are Ghosts
The Great British Ghost Hunt
Best True Ghost Stories
In Search of Ghosts
European Ghosts
Where the Ghosts Are
Yankee Ghosts

Life After Death, Reincarnation, and ESP

Beyond This Life
Born Again
Patterns of Destiny
ESP and You
The Truth About ESP
The Handbook of Parapsychology
Predictions: Fact or Fallacy?
The Prophets Speak
Psychic Investigator
The Psychic World of Bishop Pike
Possessed
The Directory of the Occult
The Powers of the New Age
Elvis Speaks From the Beyond
Psychic Photography
The Psychic World of Plants
Life Beyond Life: The Evidence for Reincarnation

Healing, Dreams, Personality Expansion

Beyond Medicine
The Human Dynamo
The Psychic Side of Dreams
The Power of Hypnosis
Charismatics
How to Cope with Problems
Speed Thinking
The Vegetarian Way of Life
Astrology—What It Can Do For You
The Aquarian Age
Psycho-Ecstasy

Other Non-Fiction

The Truth About Witchcraft
The New Pagans
The Witchcraft Report
Window to the Past
Star in the East
The Ufonauts: New Facts on Extra-terrestrial Landings
Word Play
The Habsburg Curse
Murder in Amityville

Fiction/Novels

The Alchemist
Heather, Confession of a Witch
The Clairvoyant
The Entry
The Amityville Curse
The Zodiac Affairs
Circle of Love
The Red Chindvit Conspiracy
The Alchemy Deception
The Unicorn
The Secret of Amityville